SERIES

INTO HIS LOVE

WARD PATTERSON

PSALMS 101-150

D1417221

ACCENT BOOKS
Denver, Colorado

ACCENT BOOKS

A division of Accent Publications, Inc.
12100 West Sixth Avenue
P.O. Box 15337
Denver, Colorado 80215

Library of Congress Catalog Card Number 88-70858

ISBN 0-89636-240-X

INTRODUCTION

The Psalms are God's manual for praise and prayer. They are unique in Biblical literature in that they are inspired words from God that speak either about Him or are directed toward Him. In them God reveals to us divinely sanctioned patterns for adoration and praise.

This book grew out of a deep, personal need. I was aware that adoration and praise were to be a part of my prayer life. But I found that I did not really possess a vocabulary of praise. I tried to praise God in my prayers, but within a few minutes I invariably ran out of things to say about God to God. I had little trouble with intercession and petition. I could ask for things for others and for myself. Worship and thanksgiving, however, were another matter.

It dawned on me, at length, that I needed some schooling in the art of creative worship and praise. I needed some help with my prayer life. I needed to learn how to see the world as the psalmists saw it. I needed to learn how to speak to God about Himself.

With this in mind, I set about turning the Psalms into prayers. Many, of course, are already written as prayers. They are written in the second person and address God. Many others, however, are written in the third person and speak to others about God. I did not intend to paraphrase the Psalms so much as to elaborate on them. I wanted to personalize them, to make them relevant to the world I live in, to put them into words of my understanding. I did not seek to write them with an abundance of metaphor and simile. Rather, I wanted to take the metaphors already in the Psalms and elaborate upon their meanings. Using the Psalms as my inspiration, I wanted to let my mind rove in whatever direction it chose as I meditated on the words and allowed the thoughts of the psalm to send my thoughts flying wherever they would go.

I used a number of different versions as the basis for these prayer psalms. I made no attempt to record every concept in the psalm under consideration. Nor did I always use the order of the original. The long psalms were sometimes condensed, the short ones expanded. The purpose of the exercise was devotional. I did not struggle for exegetical meaning so much as I sought devotional enlightenment.

My purpose, in the beginning, was purely private. I wanted merely to experiment with a writing discipline that would improve my prayer life. I found that I enjoyed the project tremendously. Many times I could not stop with one or two psalms a day. The more I turned my mind to the nature of God, the more I wanted to praise Him. And the more I worked with His word, the more I delighted in it. The project became as addictive to me as jogging to a health nut. If I missed a day, I was disappointed. I looked forward each morning to the opportunity to sit down with my basement computer and speak God's words back to Him.

I began sharing my work with others. The wide range of emotions expressed in the Psalms guaranteed that the prayers would speak to a wide variety of human need. I began enclosing them in letters to friends. I began to read some as a part of our student worship services. Something, however, began to change as I began to use the prayers rhetorically. I had begun the project for private reasons, but more and more I began to use the psalms publicly. Almost without noticing it, I began to think of what others might think of my work more than what God would think of it. I began, I must confess, to pray to be heard of men. It was turning into a writing project rather than a personal devotional exercise. And in so doing, it began losing some of its life and joy. While still feeling that the prayers might minister to others, I tried to remind myself that they were being addressed primarily to God and that my fundamental motive was to please Him.

The psalm/prayers in this book are published in hope that they will be used for private prayer and for public reading. I also hope that they will be used for comfort and encouragement. But most of all, I hope that they will cause others to undertake this same prayer project for themselves.

The psalmists are often discouraged and bewildered, but the light of faith invariably breaks through the darkness of doubt and disappointment. God is not offended by our honest expressions of discouragement and bewilderment. It is hoped that the prayers of this book will minister to you in the unpredictable, changing circumstances of your life, and that they will enable you to speak to God honestly and openly about the tensions as well as the joys of your life.

PSALM 101

O Lord, I am overcome with wonder
at the way You combine love and justice.
Help me to return Your love and to live uprightly.
I want You to be sovereign in every aspect of my life.
I want to be blameless before You.

Father, help me to have a pure heart.
Help me to focus my attention on holy things.
Keep me from lust,
from evil fantasies,
from sinful literature,
and from immoral cravings.
Help me to fill my mind with You and Your ways.
Give me a revulsion for evil.
Rid me of corrupt passions.
Protect me from faithlessness.
Help me to choose my friendships
in such a way that I will not compromise with wickedness.
Help me to speak out against all perversions of truth.
Help me to expose deceit and slander for what they are.
Help me to resist the proud and haughty.
Help me to give attention to the good,
to seek the companionship of the righteous,
to enjoy the company of the wholesome,
to surround myself with those who love You.
Keep me from becoming cozy with the wicked.
Help me to renew daily my commitment to You.
Help me to stand for right,
whether or not it is popular.
Help me to be an example of faithfulness,
speaking out for Your righteousness,
defending the good names of Your people,
working against corruption and depravity.
Help me to accomplish this, O Father,
through Your grace
and the gift of Your holy Son, Jesus.

O Lord, be sovereign in every aspect of my life.
I want to be blameless before You.

AMEN

PSALM 102

O Lord, I feel miserable.
   This is one of the worst periods in my life.
      I need Your help and consolation.
   Please respond to my prayer.
      Please listen to my request for deliverance.
         Please don't let this situation continue indefinitely.
   Listen as I pour out my distress to You.
      Have compassion and come to my aid soon, dear Lord.

You know how low I feel,
   how useless,
      how vulnerable,
         how transient,
            how pained,
               how heartbroken,
                  how burned out,
                     how lonely,
                        how blighted,
                           how withered,
                              how starved,
                                 how desolate,
                                    how abused,
                                       how abandoned,
                                          how useless.
I can't eat!
   I weep over everything and nothing.
      I waste away in solitude.
         I ache in the depths of my heart.

I can't sleep!
   I lie awake thinking of all my troubles,
      longing for what can be no more,
         knowing my poverty of spirit.

I'm frightened.
   I don't have a purpose anymore.

Nothing turns my thoughts away from my difficulties.
   My mind is like a tape recorder stuck in fast forward,
      racing ahead amidst a babel of noises.
         I'm out of control.
   I can't face the loneliness and solitude of the night.
   And the daytime holds no consolation either.
   I'm surrounded by people who don't care about my depression,
      or, worse yet, those who add to it with every comment.
   I'm defeated and dispirited,
      without noble purpose or dreams.
   Everything seems to be coming apart around me.
      I have no energy,
         no confidence,
            no joy,
               no sense of Your nearness.

Food I used to like is tasteless in my mouth.
   Your words are unreadable through my tears.
I live in a world without sunshine.
   I feel as if I'm withering, dying.
I feel as if You've abandoned me,
   that You've thrown me aside like a filthy rag,
      that You've judged me
         and found me unworthy of Your compassion.

Lord, You know there is not much in me just now to love.
   You know how difficult it is for me
      even to pour out my discouragement and fear
         to You honestly, openly.
   I'd like to put on a positive front
      and smile and repeat pious platitudes
         about how wonderful everything is.
   I'd like to cover my wounds with the bandaids
      of possibility thinking and optimistic sloganeering,
         but, quite frankly, I'm too devastated for any of that.
My life seems so short,
   so fragile,
      so futile,
         so inconsequential.

But You, O Father, are eternal.
You will be here long after I have vanished from the scene.
Though my problems seem so large in my mind,
they endure for only a split second of time
when viewed in the light of eternity.

You rule with compassion and love,
whether I realize it just now or not.
Unlike me, You are not subject to ups and downs,
ebbs and flows,
success and failure,
hope and hopelessness.

You are dependable,
glorious,
loving,
true to Your Word.

You do not forsake those who have put their trust in You.
There may be times of desolation
such as I am experiencing now,
but there will also come times
of restoration and renewal.
Everything lies in Your hands.
You will turn things around in Your own good time,
if I remain faithful and loyal to You.
You have not forgotten what is needed in my life.
You will raise me up from the dust of defeat
and rebuild the foundation of my life.

Though I am insignificant in so many ways,
You demonstrate Your loving nature to me and through me,
so that the world may know of Your glory.

I know that You hear the prayers
lifted from broken and bewildered hearts.
Sometimes I get to thinking that I've got
to have everything nicely together
to be acceptable to You.

Yet, I'm still learning that You are glorified in weakness
and that You delight in helping the destitute.
You don't reject me in my despair.
Rather, You reach out to my poverty with Your riches.
You lavish Your strength upon me
when I am least worthy of Your attention.
You teach me in times like this
that You alone are unwaveringly loving throughout eternity.

I wish I could write all this down
so that others might profit
from what I am learning in this awful situation.
I wish others who experience loss,
and failure,
and disappointment,
and personal tragedy,
could learn, as I am learning,
that relief does not come in liquor bottles,
or tranquilizers,
or Freudian therapy,
or revenge,
or rebellion,
or bitterness,
or suicide.
It comes from You and You alone!

You see my distress.
You hear my groans of agony.
You come to my aid
and liberate me from the thoughts and feelings
that hold me captive.
You free me from the fear of death.
You give me hope and confidence for the future.

O Father, when I think of You,
my troubles take on a new perspective.
I know I can endure and conquer
if I allow You to handle
the deep agonies of my life.

If I truly praise You,
 I will know Your deliverance.
  If I worship You sincerely,
   I will experience Your compassion.

It is hard for me to pray just now.
 You know that as well as I do.
And it is hard for me to praise You just now.
 But I will try.
  I know that You will not ignore me.

I suppose I should be thankful for this time.
 It is surely showing me how much I need You.
  This emptiness and awful fear
   are teaching me lessons about my mortality.
 There is no way I can play "God" anymore.
  I'm being taught that everything is beyond my control.
  I'm learning that my days are numbered.

I'm learning to trust You,
 for You are without beginning or end.
  You laid the foundations of the earth.
   You created the universe,
    and You keep it going
     by Your infinite wisdom and might.

To one who hung the stars in the heavens
 and set the earth spinning in space,
  my little problems must seem pretty simple.
You made everything that is,
 and You will remain after
  all created things vanish away.
In Your time, You will bring an end
 to all material reality as I know it.

I can't put my hope in anyone but You.
 I can't rely on anything that I can possess
  or store,
   or buy and sell.

I can't give meaning to my life
  by my own intelligence,
    or ingenuity,
      or resilient nature.
But I can share eternity with You.
  You are not subject to entropy,
    decay,
      or obsolescence.
  You are eternally the same;
    You are beyond the reach of time;
    You exist forever.

And the wonder of it all
  is that I can experience eternal life.
    In Your presence forever,
      I can know victorious,
        unending life.
If I seek You,
  You will make Yourself known to me,
    and I will find a place free from earthly turmoil.

Father, I feel so much better!
  I came to You thinking only of my pain.
    Thank You for turning my mind
      to Your eternal nature
        and magnificent concern
          for the welfare of Your creatures.

I asked You to hear my prayer for help
  and to answer it quickly.
Thank You, Lord, for doing precisely that!

AMEN

PSALM 103

With all that I am—
  my heart,
    my mind,
      and my soul—
        I want to praise You, O Lord.
I praise You for Your benefits to me,
  benefits I want to keep constantly in my consciousness.
Foremost among them is the fact that You forgave my sins.
  How wonderful that is to me!
    I scarcely know how to express
      my thanksgiving for Your redemption.

From You come physical and spiritual healing,
  sustenance and rejuvenation.
I am destined for death, but You give me life.
  You deal with me in love,
    kindness, and mercy.
I thank You that You make me soar with the eagles,
  not squirm with the worms.
    You lift my eyes to the high places
      and give me strength to climb.
You do not forget the oppressed of this world,
  the victims of injustice and wickedness.

Thank You for revealing Your nature and will
  through the patriarchs and prophets,
    so that I may know You as You truly are.
Thank You for choosing a people through whom
  to bring about reconciliation and redemption.

Lord, I just want to thank You for Your mercy,
  Your grace,
    and Your patience.
I know that You hate wickedness,
  and I thank You for not dealing with me
    as my sinfulness deserves.

Your mercy is beyond my understanding.
  To me, it is like an infinite number,
    or the speed of light,
      or the expanse of the universe.
As far as the east is from the west,
  You have separated my transgressions from me.
In Your all-encompassing,
  all-creating,
    all-understanding,
      eternal nature,
        You treat me like a father treats his child.
  You empathize with me,
    love me,
      hold me,
        and wrap Your loving arms around me.
You have wonderful plans for me,
  yet You understand my human limitations.
    You know me inside out—
      my inadequacies,
        my mortality.
  Life goes so fast,
    and we comprehend so little, so late.
  I am like a flower,
    blooming for a short time,
      then withering away.
  I am like a sea breeze,
    felt for a brief moment,
      then dissipating and dying away.

But You are so different.
  You are eternal.
    You are everlasting to everlasting.
      Your mercy never changes,
        disappears,
          withers,
            wears out,
              or grows old.
You have revealed Yourself through promises and commands.
  You have destined me for Your eternal home in the heavens.

In wonder I join with the angels
who day and night praise Your name.
Help me, in my world, to be like they are in theirs—
constantly in tune with You and Your will.

O Lord, I join with the celestial choirs to bless Your name.
I join with the angels around Your throne to glorify Your name.
I join with those throughout the world
who do Your bidding and magnify Your name.
I join with the stars in the heavens,
with the creatures of the oceans,
with the granite of the mountains,
with the trees of the forest,
with the waters of the rivers,
with the largest animals
and the smallest creeping things,
with the mists and clouds,
and with the smoke and fire,
To praise Your glorious name!

You have made me for this very purpose,
to join in the praise songs of all creation.

Let all that is within me bless Your name, O Lord Most High.
AMEN

PSALM 104

O Lord, You are my king!
Your greatness is beyond my comprehension.
You are clothed in splendor and majesty.
You are covered by dazzling light.
The heavens are Your royal canopy.
The clouds are Your royal chariot.
You ride with the swiftness of the wind.
You send Your messages with the gale
and Your commands with the lightning bolt.
Fire is Your servant.

You are a builder of extraordinary accomplishment.
You set the earth on its foundations.
You cover it with the great, swelling seas.
You heap up mountains.
You send rain from Your heavenly cistern.
You control tides and currents.
You create mountain streams and thunderous waterfalls.
You put everything in its place.
You control the whole earth.

You rule over this world with wisdom.
You give water to the springs and rivers
so that Your creatures may be refreshed.
You provide sanctuary for the birds of the sky.
Their songs of contentment are heard in the trees.
You bring renewal with the spring rains.
The earth bursts to life at Your command.
You give man his food,
making the grass grow for his cattle
and the seed sprout for his crops.
Your harvest brings joy and gladness.
You make the vine heavy with succulent fruit.
You cover the hillsides with olive trees.
You nourish the cedars of the mountains.
You ripen the grain in the fields.

How lovely and peaceful are Your royal gardens.
  Birds nest in the trees,
    wild goats roam the high mountains,
      rabbits hide in the crags and crevices.

All things are subject to Your rule.
  The moon waxes and wanes;
    the sun rises and sets.
  All things have their times and seasons.
    The wild beasts come alive in the night.
      The lions roar and are fed from Your hand.
      Daybreak comes and they rest in their dens.
Then it is man's turn to labor through the daylight hours.

It is impossible to comprehend the complexity of Your works.
  Only Your wisdom could create and control them.
    The earth is full of living creatures,
      all bearing the mark of Your creative mind and hand.
The sea swarms with complex living things
  that we pass over so ignorantly in our ships.
    Below us is a world of infinite beauty and intriguing design.
    All things in this dark, teeming world of the sea
      look to You for survival.
    You provide every tiny tropical fish with what it needs to live,
      and You set the table for the mighty blue whale as well.
In an infinite cycle of life and death,
    You prescribe their numbers and control their appetites
      so that the balance of nature may be maintained.
      You set the time and place
        of their deaths and their replenishment.
You keep everything in balance,
  living,
    dying,
      feeding,
        growing,
          preying,
            spawning,
              hatching,
                and mating.

O Mighty God, Your glory is everywhere.
  May it be recognized and proclaimed forever.
    May Your creation praise You and magnify Your name.
  May we who are in Your image bring You joy.
You are sovereign over all the earth and its inhabitants.
  The earth trembles at Your glance;
    it smokes at Your touch.

Father, let me be numbered among Your loyal subjects.
  Help me to sing songs of Your greatness.
    Help me to acknowledge Your rule in my life.
      Help me to sing of Your glory as long as I live.
  Let my eyes be open to Your mighty works.
    Let my thoughts be continually of You.
      Let my joy spring from my relationship with You.
        May I forsake the way of sin
          and be Your loyal subject forever.

My soul praises You, my Lord and my King.

AMEN

PSALM 105

I want to give thanks to You, O Lord.
　I want to call upon Your name,
　　for You alone are worthy of my praise.
　I want to speak of Your glorious deeds
　　to all who inhabit the earth.
　I want to broadcast Your greatness.
　　I want to sing of Your majesty,
　　　to find my daily joy in You,
　　　　to glory in Your name forevermore.
My heart longs for Your strength and power in my life.
　I yearn for Your direction and approval.

I savor the memory of Your marvelous works
　in the history of Israel.
I remember Your miraculous provision for them,
　Your incomparable commandments,
　　Your wonderful protection.
How marvelous it is to be among those You have chosen.
　How strengthening to be tried and tested for Your purposes.
　　How reassuring to know that You turn calamities to good.
　　How amazing to be protected by Your strength.
　　　How joyful to be exalted by Your providence.
　　　　How wonderful to be instructed by Your wisdom.
How overwhelming to be encouraged in the midst of danger.
　How wonderful to see Your hand at work in raising up leaders.
　　How awesome to witness Your wonders and miracles.
　　　How astonishing to observe Your control over nature.
　　　How startling to perceive the expenditure
　　　　of Your power on my behalf.
How reassuring to experience Your vitality.
　How welcome to receive Your deliverance.
　　How pleasant to experience Your freedom.
　　　How comforting to be covered by Your presence,
　　　　How illuminating to be led by Your light.
It is delicious to be fed at Your table and
　refreshing to drink from Your living water.

You always keep Your promises.
    You establish the habitation of those who trust in You.
        You produce joy and singing.
You are always at work in the lives of Your chosen,
    leading,
        prompting,
            judging,
                providing,
                    strengthening,
                        protecting,
                            revitalizing,
                                rescuing,
                                    prodding,
                                        delivering,
                                            gladdening,
                                                covering,
                                                    enlightening,
                                                        satisfying,
                                                            remembering,
                                                                blessing.
You give us benefits we do not deserve.
    You give us fruitfulness beyond our labors.
        You give us contentment exceeding our fondest desires.

All of this should cause us to follow Your ways,
    to make us intent upon keeping Your commandments,
        and to produce firm commitment to Your directives.

That is my desire, O Lord.
    Help me, by Your strength, to so live
        that my obedience is a continual message of praise to You.
                                                        AMEN

PSALM 106

O Father, Your goodness inspires my praise.
  Your love elicits my thanksgiving.
    Your mighty deeds defy description.
    Your mercy endures forever.
O God, I am happy when I do what is right.
  I am blessed when I pursue justice.
Show Your favor in my times of need.
  Save me from the things that frighten.
    Fill me with the joy of my salvation.

You know how susceptible to sin I am.
  I am like the people of Israel in my waywardness.
    I turn to wickedness and disobedience
      just as they did when You came to them in Egypt.
    They were forgetful of Your lovingkindness.
    They rebelled against Your leading.
Yet, You did not utterly forsake them.
    You preserved them for the sake of Your good name.
    You demonstrated Your power on their behalf.
      You split the Red Sea and led them to safety.
      You delivered them with a mighty hand
      from the power of their enemies.
        You saved them and redeemed them.

Oh, at the moment of Your mighty deliverance,
  they rejoiced in You.
    They sang Your praise with sincere hearts.
    They believed Your promises.
      They acknowledged Your glorious triumph.
But, like me, they were so forgetful.
  They forgot how You destroyed their enemies.
    They paid no attention to Your counsel.
    They surrendered to their cravings
    and doubted Your goodness.
So You let them have what they desired
  and delivered them to devastation.

They were restless and rebellious.
    They didn't like to follow Your appointed leaders.
        They worshiped idols that they made themselves.
    They refused to learn from Your discipline.
        They forgot that it was You who made them significant.
    They did not remember Your great wonders of deliverance.
It was only the intercession of Moses
    that held back the destruction they deserved.
        He stood in the breach and pled for his ungrateful people.

You just couldn't please them.
    They grumbled against Your leading.
    They despised the land You gave them.
And so You departed from them.
    You scattered them;
        You gave them over to what they desired.
    They opened their hearts to the degradation of false worship.
    They set their feet on the road of wickedness.

You could not help but be angry with them.
    They refused to trust Your provision.
        They rebelled against Your Spirit.
            They vexed Moses and became a cause of sin in his life.
    They refused to obey Your command
        to destroy the inhabitants of the promised land.
    They adopted the customs of the Canaanites
        and were corrupted by their idolatry.
    They compromised their integrity
        and even joined in human sacrifice.
    They degraded,
        defiled,
            and prostituted themselves.

You were justly angry with them.
    They had rejected Your rule over their lives.
    They had renounced Your inheritance.
So You delivered them up to their enemies.
    You did not come to their aid in battle.
        You allowed them to fall by their own weakness.

There were many occasions when You returned to help them,
but they never seemed to learn the relationship
between faithfulness and blessing.
And even though You allowed them to fail,
You never completely abandoned them.
For the sake of Your covenant,
You reached out to them in love.
You caused their captors to have compassion on them.
You brought them back from captivity.
You saved them from annihilation among the nations.

Father, I see in all this such a parallel to my own life.
You have done great and wonderful things for me.
You have delivered me from the bondage of sin.
You have provided for my physical and spiritual wellbeing.
You have given me Your statutes to guide my decisions.
Yet, I am often blind to Your miracles.
I rebel against Your authority.
I wander off after false gods.
I complain against Your restraints.
I defile myself with wickedness.
I experience defeat and humiliation.

Thank You, Father, for not forsaking me when I forsake You.
I thank You for being eager for my return.
I thank You for reaching out to me in love.
I thank You for continuing to watch over me with compassion.
I thank You for hearing my anguished prayers for help.

I praise You, O God.
I give thanks to Your holy name.
I glory in Your presence.
I rejoice in Your everlasting love.

AMEN

PSALM 107

O Lord, You are a God of goodness and love.
  I delight in speaking of Your deliverance and redemption.
   You were with the desert wanderers.
    In the face of deathly hunger and thirst,
     You led them through the wilderness
      to a strong, safe place of settlement.
  You slaked their thirst and satisfied their hunger.
   Your unfailing love reached out to their every need.

O God, You broke down the gates and bars of the imprisoned.
  You came to the aid of those who sat in dungeons,
   suffering in chains because of their rebellion against You.
  Though they had despised Your counsel,
   when they cried out in repentance,
    You delivered them from their distress.
  You broke their chains
   and threw open the barred doors that held them.

You rescued those who were ill.
  It was because of rebellion and iniquity that
   they suffered affliction.
    They could not eat.
     They despaired of life itself.
  But when they prayed in their time of trouble,
   You heard and saved them.
  You spoke and they were healed.
   You reached out and rescued them from death.

You guided to safe harbor those in terror on the sea.
  They went out in their ships,
   seeking trade with strange and distant lands.
  They were caught in the teeth of the tempest;
   their ships were thrown high into the air,
    then dashed into the depths of destruction.
  They lost all courage in the terror of the storm.
   They had no idea how to save themselves.

At their prayer, however, You stilled the storm,
   hushed the waves,
      and calmed the sea.
In all these extreme circumstances,
   You hearkened to the cry of their troubled spirits.
      You delivered them from the things that threatened them.
And they responded with thanksgiving
   for Your unfailing love and Your wondrous deeds among them.

Help me, O Father, to depend on You for my needs.
   Help me to realize that You hear my cries for deliverance.
      Help me to experience Your preservation.
         Help me to give thanks for Your indescribable love.
            Help me to be thankful for Your marvelous deeds.

You are a God who turns rivers into deserts,
   springs into dry holes,
      and fertile land into wasteland
         for those who live in wickedness.
And You turn deserts into lush oases,
   dry gulleys into flowing streams,
      and desolate places into fertile fields,
         for those who live in goodness and truth.

You bring calamity and sorrow to those who forsake You.
   You humble them by the oppression of their enemies.
      You have no respect for their nobility,
         but send them wandering the trackless wasteland.
Yet, those who seek to live uprightly receive Your blessing.
   You come to the aid of the needy.
      You help the lowly at every turn.
   You make very clear Your blessings.

Father, give me wisdom as I consider Your great love.
   Let me heed the lessons that You would teach me.
You are a God who responds
   to the repentant and contrite heart.
   You are a God who cares about human need
      . . . about my need.

You are a God of love and compassion.
　You are a God of goodness and deliverance.
　　You are a God of healing and peace.
　　　You are a God of blessing and joy.

You satisfy as no other person or thing can!
　Let me tell of Your works
　　with words and songs of gladness.

AMEN

PSALM 108

O God, I want one thing—
  to trust in You with all my heart and mind.
    I want to stand firm in my resolve,
      to put You first in all my thoughts and affections.

I delight in singing Your greatness—
  not just mouthing words of adoration
    but opening my innermost being to Your glory.
Give me a steadfast heart,
  a joyous heart,
    a singing heart.
I love music
  for it awakens in me
    the desire to praise You.

O Lord, I love to see the sunrise, too.
  It reminds me that each new day is the gift of Your hand.
    I love to walk by a lake
      and see the red of the dawn
        reflected on its mirror surface.
    I love to walk through a woods
      as the new day begins
        and watch the chipmunks
          scurrying about on their appointed tasks.
    I love to pray in the early hours,
      as darkness gives way to light,
        and to think of the glory of resurrection morn
          when Jesus turned the defeat of death
            into the triumph of new life.
    When I pray at the beginning of the day,
      this sets me in the right direction
        and reminds me of Your presence in all my affairs.
          As I pour out my frustrations,
            my disillusionments, my trials,
              my fears, my dreams,
                and my failures,
          I receive Your peace and consolation.

O Lord, in this world
 where so many nations and peoples do not know You,
  I want to be at least one voice of adoration.
 Help me to reach out
  both in this country
   and in the nations of the world
    with the message of Your abiding love.

Your love is higher than the heavens.
 Your faithfulness is broader than the firmament.
  Your rule is supreme in the heavens.
It extends, as well, through all the earth.
 Help me to so exalt Your name by word and deed
  that all may know Your greatness and love.

Father, each day I need Your help.
 I need Your wisdom,
  lest I be consumed by foolish desires.
 I need Your strength,
  lest I be overpowered by the forces of evil.
 I need Your deliverance,
  lest I be shackled by enslaving sin.
 I need Your sanctuary,
  lest I become a casualty to the worldliness of my time.

Father, You control all things.
 You put nations in their places.
  You form their natural boundaries,
   dictate their destinies,
    and give them the resources they develop.
 You establish their climates
  and rule over their harvests.
Nations exist by Your grace.
 They boast of their independence
  and pride themselves in their governments,
   but You are sovereign over them all.

O God, I know all this.
 Yet, I sometimes think that I am in control.

I begin to believe that everything is mine
  to manipulate for my benefit.
    I get arrogant in my pride
      and think that I can bring about
        the things I desire.
  Or I turn my eyes away from Your might
    and become frightened by the enemies that surround me.
You alone are the source of lasting satisfaction,
  the hope of eternal life.
    I know that You are my help in every need,
      my strength in every battle,
        my companion in every difficulty.

Please be with me today.
  Don't reject me because of my iniquities.
    Forgive my sins
      and create right attitudes in me.

AMEN

PSALM 109

O Father, there are times when I want revenge.
  I'm fed up with the treatment meted out to me
    by wicked men and women.
  I just cannot tolerate injustice any longer.
    My soul cries, "It is enough!
      Give evildoers what they deserve!"

O God, this is one of those times!
  I feel maligned,
    hated,
      surrounded,
        attacked,
          lied about,
            spitefully used,
              hounded,
                cursed,
                  accused,
                    and betrayed.
My enemies are like birds of prey,
  ripping to pieces a dead carcass.
    They hover about,
      then descend on me to tear and destroy.
When I respond to my enemies with friendship,
  they treat it as weakness.
    They return my kindness with hate and violence.

O Father, I try to live as a person of prayer.
  I try to treat everyone I meet
    with goodness and honesty.
      But it is so hard, sometimes, Lord.
Some people seem bent on my downfall.
  They oppose and accuse
    and can't wait to destroy my reputation.
  They want to silence my prayers and twist my words,
    thwart my influence,
      and bring me down to disgrace and death.

They want evil to befall both me and my children.
They want my family to be in want
and my home to be in ruins.
They'd like to see me in utter poverty.
They would delight if all I have was taken from me.
They'd love to see me condemned and lost eternally.
They want my sins and faults to be remembered
and my goodness to be blotted out.
Such people seem to abound on this earth—
never doing a kindness if they can devise a scheme
to take advantage of the poor,
never showing compassion,
never helping the needy or brokenhearted.

Father, turn their curses back on them.
Give them the terrible things they wish on others.
May their evil words and thoughts
clothe them like a shroud
and strangle them in their own blasphemies.

O Father, vindicate the righteous.
Silence the slander of the wicked.
Close the mouths of the devourers.
Unleash Your wrath upon the accusers and abusers.

Help me, Father, to be different from those I despise.
Be sovereign in my thoughts and deeds.
Treat me with Your love and kindness
and deliver me from evil.

You know, O Father, how much I need You!
I am impoverished, incapable,
downcast, faint,
and derided.
I have no sense of permanence,
stability,
purpose,
or hope.
I feel so conspicuous and broken.

O Lord, please help me!
  Save me by Your grace!
    Let my enemies know You are with me!
     Bless my life!
      Defend my honor!
       Bring joy to my heart!
        Deliver me from my accusers!
I will ever thank You for what You have done in my life.
I will lead a great company in proclaiming Your praise.

Father, I know that You stand with me in my need.
  You vindicate the righteous and condemn the wicked.
    I can trust You with my discouragement
     and rely on You to take care of my enemies.

Father, vengeance is Yours.
  I know it is not up to me
    to cause the downfall of my adversaries.
  It is all in Your hands.
    You will do what is right and best.

But I just want You to know how I feel.

AMEN

PSALM 110

O God, today I contemplate
the wonder of Your presence in Christ Jesus.
You are one and yet separate.
He sits at Your right hand,
victorious ruler over all.
He has defeated all the forces of evil,
having nailed them to His cross.
He has dealt a mortal blow
to the pretensions of Satan.

Thank You for Jesus,
my king and high priest.
He has extended His rule throughout the whole earth.
He is surrounded by all the hosts of heaven.

He is the great high priest,
without beginning and without end,
holy,
blameless,
pure,
sinless,
exalted above the heavens.
He intercedes for me before Your throne.
He bears witness to Your words of life.
He has made the sacrifice of His own blood for my sins.

Christ reigns victorious!
He sits in power and glory at Your right hand.
He will judge all nations and all peoples.
All earthly power is subject to Him.
He has all authority.

Thank You for Jesus Christ,
my Savior,
and my sovereign Lord.

AMEN

PSALM 111

O Father, how wonderful it is
  to ponder Your greatness!
    It fills me with awe
      to meditate upon Your mighty works.
  Your wonders are everywhere.
    Your goodness encompasses my world.
     Your glorious acts surround me.

O Father, there is nothing I would rather do than praise You.
  I love to speak of You in the worship assembly.
    I delight in sharing my trust in You.
  I look forward to every opportunity
    for corporate worship and praise.

Your righteousness is incomparable.
  Your goodness is everlasting.
    Your glory is never dimmed.
      Your majesty is without compare.
        Your compassion is unlimited.
        Your grace is all-sufficient.
          Your providence is bountiful.
          Your faithfulness is steadfast.
            Your precepts are trustworthy.
            Your redemption is eternal.
            Your promises are sure.
            Your power is absolute.
            Your justice is true.

I find it impossible to live in this world
  without being reminded with every breath
    of Your tender love and concern for me.
  You put food on my table.
    You give me hope in an alien world.
      You bless me in thousands of ways.
        You stand by me when I stand with you
        and even when I don't.

You give me victory when I rely upon Your power.
  You treat me with justice.
    You strengthen me in all my difficulties.
      You lead me by Your Word.
Your ways are always dependable.
  You call me to a relationship of trust and obedience.
    You cleanse me from my sins.
      You give me freedom and life.
        I am never lost if I follow You.
Help me to be faithful and upright.
  Help me to walk in Your wisdom.
    Help me to respect and follow Your commands.
      Help me to praise You fully and deeply.

Father, Your name is above every name.
  There is no one else like You
    in holiness,
      in faithfulness,
        in righteousness,
          in graciousness,
            in compassion,
              in power,
                in justice,
                  in trustworthiness,
                    in steadfastness,
                      in glory,
                        in majesty,
                          and in wisdom.

Help me, Father, to fear You.
  Help me to hold you in proper awe.
    Help me to respect and honor You.
      Help me to praise You with obedience as well as words.
Father, help me to live my life in wisdom—
  honoring You,
    obeying You,
      praising You as I ought!
O Father, how wonderful it is to meditate on Your greatness!
AMEN

PSALM 112

I will praise You, Lord.
I have set my course;
I have determined
to order my life
by Your commandments.

If I am Your child,
You will give strength.
Your blessings will fill my days
and comfort my nights.
Your riches will fill my life,
and I will know no want.
Your righteousness will overarch me,
and I will know eternal values.
You light the path of the upright.
You deal with me in compassion,
righteousness,
and grace.
You guide my affairs with wisdom.
You keep my life on a firm foundation.
You never forget me.

I need not fear the daily news.
I am not tossed about by anxiety,
for my heart is fixed on You.
I don't need to fret and worry
or struggle to impose my will on others.
You provide me with resources
—and the desire—
to help others in need.

I know that You and I will be together
long after the taunts of the wicked are silenced.
Their derision does not bother me.
They cannot understand my contentment,
my peace, or my hope.

I will praise You, Lord,
  for Your commandments,
    for Your blessings,
      for Your riches,
        for Your righteousness,
          for Your light,
            for Your grace,
              for Your compassion,
                for Your guidance,
                  for Your strength,
                    for Your deliverance,
                      for Your fulfillment,
                        and for Your consolation.
You have honored me with Your love.
I will honor You with my praise.

AMEN

PSALM 113

I want to praise You, O Lord.
  I want to join all Your servants
  in praising Your name.
  Your name is to be honored
  now and forevermore.

Your name is to be praised from sunrise to sunset,
  for You are exalted above all—
    above all political systems,
      above all power and authority,
        above all physical and natural phenomena.

Though You dwell on high,
  You humble Yourself to be concerned
  with things of this earth.
  You lift up the poor and needy
  from their frustration and despair.
  You place them on the throne of princes
  and make them glad with Your prosperity.
  You bring life to the barren
  and joy to the depressed.

I will praise You, O Lord,
  for Your magnificence,
    for Your love,
      for Your restoration,
        for Your exaltation,
          for Your provision,
            and for Your joy.

I will praise You, O Lord,
  with gladness
    and honor
      as long as I have breath!

AMEN

PSALM 114

Dear Lord,
  You are a God who acts in human history.
You are not some distant first cause
  or some alien being.
You demonstrated Your power
  and Your concern
    when You brought the Israelites
      out of slavery in Egypt.
You chose to dwell with the outcast and downtrodden.
  You singled out the disinherited and dispirited
    for a special relationship with You.

Such are Your ways, O Lord.
  You set the captives free.
    You make Your dwellingplace with the weak.
    You rule among the lowly.

Thank You for liberating me
  from the bondage of sin.
Thank You for leading me
  into newness by Your mighty hand.
Thank You for making my heart Your sanctuary
  and exercising Your power through my life.

The Israelites marveled as You moved the earth
  and the waters for their benefit.
You turned stone into water
  so that they might drink and be refreshed.
You parted the Jordan before the forces of Joshua.
  The earth shook beneath their feet
    as You threw about the mountains and the hills.
How mighty,
  how involved,
    how dramatic,
    how faithful
      You are!

O Liberator,
   free me from the things that enslave me.
O Mover of Mountains,
   break down the obstacles and barriers of my life.
O Parter of Seas,
   cause me to walk confidently in the face of
      the things that threaten to overwhelm my joy in You.

Help me to know Your faithful watchcare
   in the difficulties of my existence.
Help me to trust You in the face of
   problems that seem insurmountable.
Help me to lift up my eyes to You
   when I find myself in the tight places,
     the hopeless situations,
       the incomprehensible jams,
         the frightening blind alleys,
          the bewildering cul-de-sacs.
Help me to remember Israel when I feel
   like throwing in the sponge,
     cutting and running,
       waving the white flag,
         jumping into the lifeboats,
          throwing up my hands,
            dropping out,
              resigning from the human race.

Demonstrate Your presence to me
   in dramatic ways when necessary
     and in quiet ways when You so desire.
Turn the rocks of my life
   into springs of fresh water.
     Bring life to my barrenness,
       refreshment to my desert,
         hope to my hopelessness,
          vision to my fearful eyes.

Turn my captivities
   into reminders of deliverance.

Turn my hard places
    into occasions for thanksgiving.
Turn my fears
    into lessons in reliance.
Turn my difficulties
    into memories of Your loving care.
Turn my challenges
    into remembrances of victory.

You are a God who acts
    in human history.

Move in me.

AMEN

PSALM 115

O Lord God, all glory belongs to You.
   You are a God of love and faithfulness.
      You deal with me in compassion and understanding.
         You engulf me in Your care and surround me with good.
   Whatever significance I possess is because of You.
      You alone give me meaning.
         You alone give me confidence.
   You are a God who involves Himself in human affairs.
      You are almighty,
         all wise,
            eternally true and just.
   You inhabit the heavens,
      but You are intimately involved with life on earth.

I often make false gods and bow down to them.
   Oh, I don't carve idols of wood or stone.
      I don't cast images of animals
         or fabricate icons of precious metals.
   People who create such gods create them in human image
      so that they can use them for selfish ends.
         I'm much too sophisticated for that.
            I realize such things offer no help or hope.

Yet, I do have my own gods—
   those things that assume too much prominence in my life,
      those things that turn my attention from You,
         those things that I control and which control me.

O Father, help me to put away the paganism of my society:
   the worship of self,
      the worship of material things,
         the worship of pleasure.
   Help me, instead, to trust in You,
      to rely on You for my help,
         to depend on You for my defense.
   Help me, Father, to experience Your blessing.

O Maker of heaven and earth,
   everything is Your possession.
Nothing I hoard and barter for is truly mine.
   All things are on loan.
You've allowed me a brief span to enjoy my life on earth
   and have given me so many things to bless me.
I want to praise You while I have life within me.
   My days will end soon enough.
      I'll be silenced by the grave one day soon.
         But until then, I want to extol You
            with my whole strength.
I know that one day,
   when this life comes to an end,
      I will be able to worship You eternally.

O Lord, I praise You!
   I glorify Your name.
      I put my trust in You.
      I stand in awe before You.

You are my God,
   both now and forevermore.

AMEN

PSALM 116

O Lord, I love You so much.
　I love You for hearing my prayers.
　　You never treat me like the sinner I am.
　　　Rather, You treat me with compassion and respect.
　You pay attention to me in my distress.
　　You deliver me from the pitfalls of my life.

Father, help me to be diligent in prayer.
　I am so inconsistent,
　　lackadaisical,
　　　superficial,
　　　　routine,
　　　　　undisciplined,
　　　　　　and doubting in my prayer life.
Help me to delight in communion with You,
　to long for every opportunity to talk with You,
　　to yearn for Your friendship and approval.
Help me to be a person of prayer!

Father, I don't know why
　the discipline of prayer seems so hard for me.
　　You have already proved to me—over and over—
　　　how essential prayer is to my well-being.
There have been times when I was desperately sick.
　I didn't know where to turn or what to do.
　　I was overcome by fear and sorrow.
　　　Everything seemed out of kilter.
　　My life was falling apart.
　　　My problems were just too many,
　　　　and my resources were just too few.
　　I had exhausted all my wisdom
　　　and exerted all my strength—to no avail.
Then I turned to You
　and called out in desperation,
　　"Lord, save me!"
And You heard my prayer.

O God, You are so gracious,
  so righteous,
    so compassionate,
     so forgiving
     and so loving.
You surround the simple with Your wall of protection.
  You come to the aid of those in need.
   You save those who call out to You.

I've learned to bring all my concerns to You.
  And I've found the deliverance and rest I've longed for.
You have always showered me with good.
  You have released me from pain and grief.
   You have wiped the tears from my eyes
    and steadied my stumbling feet.
   You have renewed my vision
    and provided purpose and hope for the future.
   You have given me confidence
    that with You I can meet whatever comes into my life.

When I prayed, You delivered me from cynicism
  and disillusionment with my fellow men and women.
You put my troubles in perspective.
  You helped me to realize that the things I was facing
   were not so horrendous as I
    was making them out to be.
  You helped me to sort through the ways
   I was lying to myself and to others.
    You taught me to look at things Your way.
I am so often incapacitated by fear.
  I fear ridicule,
   embarrassment,
    helplessness,
     ignorance,
      sickness,
       death.
My dread of death seems to lurk
  behind every other fear in my life.

But You have taught me another side of death.
  You have shown me
    that there is something worse than physical death—
    the death of responsiveness to You.

  You have taught me how dear the faithful are to You.
  I have learned that the death of Your
    saints is precious in Your sight.

O Father, how You have comforted me in the face of death!
  You have freed me from the chains that shackle me—
    worry,
      sorrow,
        futility,
          hopelessness,
            despair,
              deceit,
                self-absorption,
                  purposelessness,
                    condemnation,
                      and death itself.

The more I think of these things
  the more awed by prayer I become.
    You have filled my life with so many essential—
    so many good—things!
What can I give You in return?
  I have nothing to give that is not already Yours.
    You made my life and all the things I possess.
But I can give You my praise and thanksgiving.
  I can acknowledge You as the source of my salvation.
    I can honor You with my adoration.
      I can call on Your name in prayer.
        I can influence others to follow You.
          I can dedicate my life to obeying Your will.
            I can recognize Your hand in every good thing
            and be thankful.
              I can live out my life in honesty
              and reverence before You.

O Father, You have been faithful to me.
  Help me to be faithful to you!
    Help me to apply what I have learned about prayer
      to my present and future walk with You.
        Help me to praise You
          with every meditation of my heart.
O Lord my God, help me to be a person of prayer.

AMEN

PSALM 117

I praise You, Lord!
  I want to join in a magnificent chorus
    of people from all nations of the earth,
      united in heart and voice to lift up Your name
        in joyous, loving praise.

Oh that the earth resounded with words of praise
  rather than threats of war.
Oh that the battlefields of hatred
  were transformed into meadows of peace and prayer.
Oh that the divisions of race and culture
  were bridged by common loyalty to Your name.
Oh that the selfishness of nations
  was changed into compassion for the needy.
Oh that the minds of the nations' leaders
  were focused on righteousness rather than power.
Oh that the earth resounded with words of adoration
  to Your holy name!

In a world of constant change,
  Your truth endures forever.
In a world driven by selfishness,
  Your lovingkindness is great.
In a world of broken relationships,
  Your love is constant.
In a world divided by ill will,
  Your will is altogether good.

I want to praise You, O Lord!
  Let there be a magnificent chorus
    of people from all nations of the earth,
      united in heart and voice to lift up Your name
        in joyous, loving praise.

AMEN

PSALM 118

O Lord, thank You for Your goodness,
   Your love,
      Your protection,
         Your liberation,
            Your help,
               Your strength,
                  Your salvation,
                     Your joy,
                        Your victory,
                           Your chastening,
                              Your righteousness,
                              and Your holiness.

Your love endures forever!
   Your mercy sets me free.
      Your presence comforts me.
      Your power brings me victory.

You are my refuge.
   I put my trust in You.
Unlike men, You will never let me down.
   You are eternally steadfast and sure.
In Your name I can face every obstacle,
   and overcome any foe.
No difficulty is too large;
   no problem is too complex;
      no situation is so hopeless,
         that I cannot triumph in Your name.

You are on my side.
   You are my strength.
      You are my song.
         You are my salvation.
You have done great things in my life.
   My heart overflows with songs of joy and victory.

Thank You for giving me life.

There have been times
   when I have needed Your discipline,
      but You have kept me safe through every trial.

I want everyone to know what a great God You are.
   I want to give thanks, dear Lord,
      for Who You are,
         for salvation,
            and for giving me all things to enjoy.
Help me to walk the path of righteousness.
   Help me to follow You, O Lord Jesus,
      the stone rejected by the builders.
         You are the chief cornerstone of faith.
Help me to rejoice and be glad every day of my life.

O Lord, give me true success.
   I don't need a lot of wealth
      and I don't need to be famous.
But I do want to know You.
   I want to know Your blessing.

O Lord, You are my God.
   You are the source of light and life!
      Help me to praise You with exuberance.
You are my God!
   I thank You for all You have done for me.
You are my God!
   I thank You for Your unchanging character.

Your love endures forever!
   Your mercy sets me free!
      Your presence comforts me!
         Your help brings me victory!

AMEN

PSALM 119

O Lord, how I thank You for the instruction of Your statutes.
Your law reveals the way for me to walk in blamelessness.
Help me, O Father, to obey Your commands.
Help me to walk in Your ways.
Help me to honor Your commandments in all my actions.
Help me to praise You with an upright heart.
Help me to regulate my life by Your righteous laws.
Be with me, Father,
as I attempt to walk the way of obedience.

Father, I want to live according to Your Word.
I want to order my life in purity.
I want to seek You with all my heart.
I want to make Your will
the standard for my conduct.
I know that in order to do this,
I must meditate faithfully upon Your Word.
I must treasure Your law in my heart.
I must be able to identify sin and flee from it.

O God, make me understand Your will.
Help me to internalize Your commandments.
Help me to find my greatest joy in obedience.
Help me to center my thoughts and affections on Your ways.
Help me to read Your Word consistently,
deeply,
thoughtfully,
obediently.

The greatest thing in life is to obey You.
Give me eyes to see things as You see them.
Help me to honor Your law eagerly.
It is by Your commandments that You guide me
through the uncertainties of my existence.
I know that You rebuke those who go their own way
without regard to Your statutes.

Your Word is my counsel,
  my companion,
    my delight,
      my strength,
        my understanding,
          my trust,
            my hope,
              my freedom,
                my love,
                  my meditation,
                    my comfort,
                      my salvation,
  my song,
    my portion,
      my knowledge,
        my judgment,
          my treasure,
            my joy,
              my teacher,
                my bounty,
                  my lamp,
                    my light,
                      my guide,
                        my restoration,
                          my shield,
                            my direction,
                              my roadmap,
                                my redemption,
                                  my deliverance,
                                  and my help.

I know that if I live by Your laws,
  my life will be free from futility.
No matter in what other areas I may fail,
  if I am faithful to Your decrees, I will be a victor.
    Strengthen me,
      renew me,
        teach me,
          keep me.

Be gracious to me, O Lord,
   vindicate me,
      direct me,
         comfort me,
            preserve me,
               save me,
                  accept me,
                     sustain me,
                        uphold me,
                           redeem me,
                           hear me,
                              encourage me,
                                defend me.

Father, keep me from pursuing worthless ambitions.
   Spare me from giving my life for selfish accomplishments.
     Help me to draw from your Word
       the central absolutes of my life.
   No matter what others say or do,
     I have chosen to live by Your truth.
     I am renewed by Your promises,
       redeemed by Your love.

Give me an urgency about obedience.
   Keep me resolute in my determination to be faithful.
   Preserve my delight in following Your decrees.

Your laws are righteous.
   Your statutes are trustworthy.
     Your Word is eternal.
       Your commands are boundless.
         Your decrees are wise.
           Your promises are sweet.
             Your precepts are the joy of my heart.

I take my stand with You, O God.
   Do not let evildoers prevail against me.
     Deal with me compassionately.
       Give me discernment and understanding.

Wherever Your Word is, there is light.
Free me from the blind darkness of sin.
Give me righteous indignation
against those who despise Your Word.
Fill me with a passion for Your truth.
Answer the deepest prayers of my heart.
Hear my voice in accordance with Your laws.
Renew my life to harmony with Your will.
Relieve the anguish of my spirit.
Defend and deliver me.

My heart overflows with praise
when I think of Your revelation to me.
A song comes to my lips
as I learn new truths from your Word.
My strength is renewed in the face of persecution.
I am preserved and sustained by Your righteousness.

Help me to honor You and Your commandments always
with wholehearted love and obedience!

AMEN

PSALM 120

I am disturbed, O Lord.
   The society I live in confuses and troubles me.
      I am frightened by the violence I see on the evening news.
      I am appalled by the immorality I read in the daily papers.
      I am terrified by the falsehood and "disinformation"
        that is the accepted norm of my times.
   And my own heart is so often vengeful,
      immoral, and deceitful.

Help me to break free of my sinful nature.
   Help me to live untainted by my corrupt environment.
Set my feet on a pilgrimage to the higher places of life.
   Help me to lift up my eyes to Your city of holiness.
      Help me to set my feet on the long path
        that ascends toward your sanctuary.

This world seems to live and move on lies.
   Advertisers entice me to buy the useless
      and the frivolous,
        witnesses perjure themselves,
          politicians promise anything to be elected,
            professors explain man without reference to You,
              students falsify their research and cheat on exams,
            preachers distort the Bible
              and claim visions to increase revenue.

Father, protect me from the deceptions,
   armor me against the double-dealing,
      strengthen me against the sham,
        deliver me from the charlatanism,
          save me from the frauds,
            preserve me from the prevarications.
Help me to be a person of truth,
   a person who neither misleads nor is misled.
      Help me to use my tongue to expose falsehood,
        and to call men and women to Your truth, O God.

Our nation seems so far from you, Lord.
  We claim to be a godly nation,
    but we do not pray,
      and we do not worship,
        and we do not stand up for righteousness.
  We compete,
    and we cheat.
      We grasp,
        and we fight,
          and we victimize.
  We hoard,
    and we waste,
      and we destroy,
        and we kill.
Yet we want You to bless our evil enterprises.
  We rail at You if You don't shower Your approval on us.
  We doubt You if You don't help us build our fortunes.
  We tune in the preachers who flatter our egos,
    and turn You off when You call us to repentance.

I live in a world peopled by barbarians,
  delinquents,
    degenerates,
      vandals,
        traitors,
          liars,
            courtesans,
              dope pushers,
                gun runners,
                  libertines,
                    despots,
                      anarchists,
                        terrorists,
                          swindlers,
                            thieves,
                              exploiters,
                                con artists,
                                  pimps,
                                    and conspirators.

People seem to delight in living as far
　from Your ways as possible.
　　They are restless and undisciplined.
　　　They are constantly on the move,
　　　　but are going nowhere.
　　They want the latest and the best,
　　　but they have no understanding of ultimate worth.

O Lord, help me to do more than complain.
　Help me to be part of the solution
　　instead of a contributor to the problem.
Help me to be honest about my sins.
　Help me to repent in sorrow and anticipation.
　　Help me to be at war with evil
　　　and at peace with You.
I have decided to follow You.
　to turn over the rudder of my ship to You,
　　to make You the pilot of my destiny.
I need Your help to reject the delusions of my time.
　I need a heart for peace and words of sincerity.
　　I need to stand against the current,
　　　to hold my course,
　　　　to go upriver
　　　　　toward the mooring of Your approval.

Sometimes I feel so out of step.
　I feel as if I am the only one who thinks as I do.
　　Others laugh at my squareness,
　　　and ridicule my principles;
　　　　they coax me to abandon my commitment to You.
　　They tell me that You are dead,
　　　that morals are relative,
　　　　that right is whatever makes me feel good
　　　　　or whatever the majority favors.

Yet I know, Lord, that You alone are holy
　and that Your commandments are designed for my good.
　　I know that You speak the truth in love
　　　and that is what You desire of me as well.

I know that You have not promised me an easy road.
  You have never suggested that Your people will be popular.
    You have promised a cross before a crown.
Help me to orient my conscience by Your standards,
  to conform my words and deeds to Your will.
Help me to recognize and reject the corruption
  and the pollution of this world.
Help me to be a pilgrim on the upward path.
  Help me to sing Your praise as I ascend the steep places.
    Help me to meditate on Your Word as I rest,
      and to rely on Your strong arm as I climb.
    Help me to keep my eyes fixed on You
      and to know the freedom of Your restraint.

AMEN

PSALM 121

I will seek Your help, O God.
  I will turn my eyes to You
    and know that You are my protector,
      my deliverer,
        my helper,
          my sustainer,
            my watchman,
              my keeper,
                my healer,
                  my companion,
                    my preserver,
                      my benefactor,
                        my guard,
                          my friend,
                            and my hope,
                      forever.

When I look at the mountains,
  my eyes are lifted up to Your glory.
When I look at the heavens,
  I am reminded of Your continual watchcare.
    You never sleep.
      You are never taken by surprise.
When I see a tree,
  I think of Your shade over me.
When I see the sun,
  I am reminded that You keep me from danger.
When I see the moon,
  I recall Your deliverance from fear.
You protect me from evil;
  You keep my soul from distress.

There is nowhere I can go where You are not present.
  Whether I go out or come in,
    You are with me,
      now and forevermore.

How good it is to know
   that You will not allow me to fall,
     or slip,
       or tumble from Your mighty grasp.
How good it is to know that You never grow tired.
  How good it is to be kept by You,
    to be protected by You,
      to be preserved by You.

I need not worry about where I go
   or what lies ahead for me,
     for You are my bodyguard,
       my armor,
         my provider,
          and my peace.

Thank You, Lord.

AMEN

PSALM 122

Many things fill me with anticipation, O Lord.
   There are friends I long to see,
      and places I long to visit,
         and things I long to experience.
   But there is nothing
      quite like the gladness that wells up inside me
         when I do Your will
            and know Your blessing.
For the Jews, Jerusalem was a place of joyous pilgrimage.
   It was a city that stood high on Mount Zion.
      It was the locus of prayer,
         sacrifice,
            and thanksgiving.
               It was the center of rule and judgment.
Its name means peace,
   but it knew endless war.
Yet it stood as a spiritual refuge
   and a dwellingplace of Your blessings.

The pilgrim always looked up in anticipation
   toward Jerusalem's gates and walls.
      He studied its buildings
         and was reminded by its strength
            of Your blessings throughout Israel's history.
The pilgrim's mind turned to David and Solomon
   and the glories of their kingdoms.
      He longed for at-homeness,
         sanctity,
            security,
               fellowship,
                  peace,
                     and contentment within the city's walls.

Father, during the pilgrimage of my life,
   lift up my eyes to the high places of my security in You.
      Encompass me with Your strong parapets
         and encircle me with Your mighty fortifications.

Grant me the peace of Your sanctuary.
  Grant me Your protection,
    Your shelter,
      Your freedom,
        Your blessedness.
Today I know Your ever present reality in my life.
  Today I know joy at the privilege
    of worshiping You in my church.

Help me to rejoice in my heritage as Your child.
  Help me to take pleasure in the special places
    You have hallowed in my memory
      and marked for Your honor.

AMEN

PSALM 123

Wherever I am, O Lord, my eyes turn to You.
　　Whenever I am beset by persecution and opposition,
　　　　I come to You in prayer.
　　　　　　Whenever I find myself frustrated and bewildered,
　　　　　　　　I turn my face toward heaven and seek Your help.
I'm like a child seeking the security of its mother,
　　or a slave watching for the master's command,
　　　　or a ballplayer observing the coach's signals,
　　　　　　or a suitor gazing into the eyes of his beloved,
　　　　　　　　or a young maiden longing for a glimpse of her fiance.
I come seeking Your mercy and lovingkindness,
　　Your vindication,
　　　　Your approval.
I'm overwhelmed by ridicule.
　　I'm tortured with scorn.
　　　　I've endured all I can take of contempt.
　　　　　　I've had my fill of derision.
The proud and the lazy use me as their whipping boy.
　　They look down their noses at me
　　　　and boast of their importance.
Those who disregard You also disregard me.
　　They show me no kindness.
I feel as if I can take no more!

So look on me with compassion, Lord.
　　Send me the help I need.
　　　　Be with me in this present situation
　　　　　　and silence the accusers and scoffers
　　　　　　　　once and for all.
　　You know my breaking point,
　　　　my threshhold of pain,
　　　　　　my point of no return.
　　Treat me gently,
　　　　and lovingly,
　　　　　　and mercifully, O Lord,
　　　　　　　　for I take my cues from You.

Thank you for taking my side,
   for putting to flight my accusers,
      for delivering me from derision.
I know that You are here
   and that You really care!

AMEN

PSALM 124

O Lord, if You were not with me
I would never survive.
I would be overcome by my adversaries.
I would be drowned in my troubles.
I would be swept away by my problems.

Father, I thank You for not allowing me to be overcome.
You deliver me from the snares that surround me.
You are my help in every difficulty.
You are powerful beyond my imagining.
You are the creator of all things.

I trust in You!

AMEN

PSALM 125

Lord, I want to trust in You fully.
For when I rely on You I am on solid ground.
I am surrounded by Your power and protection.
I am secure in Your dwellingplace.

O Lord, show Your goodness to me.
Help me to be upright in heart.
Help me to walk the righteous path.
Help me to know Your peace.

AMEN

PSALM 126

O Father, thank You for bringing me through the low times.
   You know that for so long I've been
     in bondage to my troubles,
       held captive by the negative forces in my life.

But now, O God, I know the joy of freedom once again.
   I prayed for this day,
     and dreamed of it—this day of restoration,
      this day of gladness.
   I have a song in my heart at last.
     There is a smile on my face
      and laughter comes easily again.
     I giggle and hum a happy tune
      as I think of the wonderful things
       You have brought about for me.

I know that You are the source of my deliverance.
   You have brought me through my difficulties
   and led me to this high place of joy.
You have flooded my life with newness,
   like a spring rain refreshing dormant plants of winter.
You have taken my tears
   and turned them into streams of gladness.
You have taken my groanings
   and turned them into songs of praise.
You have made my life fruitful and productive once again.

The time of planting and cultivating is past.
   The rigorous labors are behind me.
Now I am ready for the harvest of faithfulness.
   I just can't contain the elation I feel.

You have changed my tears into songs of joy.
   You have transformed my weeping into cries of happiness.
     You have turned my poverty of spirit
      into a bumper crop of rejoicing.

I just can't believe that I am free again!
   I just can't quite realize that my darkness
      and defeat are behind me.
All I can do is thank You.
   You have done great things for me!

AMEN

PSALM 127

O Lord, I know that You are the source of all that is good.
My life is built on the foundation of Your love.
I am secure because of Your watchcare over me.
Unless my life is oriented toward You,
it will have no lasting security.
Unless You are the center of my priorities,
nothing I do will truly prosper.

I so often think that I am the critical factor.
I set the alarm and rise early;
I labor long hours,
and read and plan,
and pride myself in my achievements.
But none of my accomplishments is truly mine.
If it weren't for You, I could do nothing at all.

By Your grace I exist and labor.
By Your strength I am protected and allowed to act.
By Your love I am given worth and value.
My accomplishments are nothing,
if You are not in them.
My sources of pride are dust,
if You are not properly praised.
You are the source of all security and contentment.
They do not come from my hours of overtime,
or the material possessions I accumulate,
or the fame I am capable of achieving.
Your faithfulness is the foundation of my life.
I can rest peacefully because I know Your love never fails.

You are the source of all satisfaction.
My family, too, is Your gift of joy to me.
Children are Your blessing to parents.
I need to remember that—
whether it is in my relationship to my parents,
or to my children.

Children bring gladness to the heart
  and a sense of fulfillment and hope.
They brighten our lives with their smiles
  and remind us of our need for Your wisdom.
They teach us the meaning of sacrificial love
  and touch the innermost emotions of our lives.
Father, thank You for the gift of children,
    and the gift of contentment that can accompany them
      if we center our homes on Your approval
        and remember to live and teach Your values.
  Help me to be that kind of child to my parents.

I need so much to trust You more fully, O Lord!
  I need so much to live within Your will!
    I need so much to see and acknowledge Your providence!

You are the source of all contentment in my life.

AMEN

PSALM 128

O Lord, thank You for Your great promise of blessing.
  You promise to bring happiness
    to those who fear You,
      love You,
        follow You,
          truly know You.
  You promise to fill them with special prosperity,
    and inner peace,
      and true well-being.
  Their lives will be fruitful,
    their children a joy to them,
      their homes a continual source of blessing.

Yet, our choices and actions have consequences.
  We can sow attitudes and deeds of life or death.
Your blessing takes us to the heights of our existence
  and fills our days with significance.
If we fear You and walk in Your ways,
  we will see a happy old age
    and our nation will know peace.

I know this, O God.
  Then why do I so often rebel?
    I seem to fear the wrong things.
      I fear for my reputation.
        I fear for my possessions.
          I fear for my life.
            I fear for my relationships.
            I fear for my loved ones.
  But I ignore You.
    I set my own course,
      decide which of Your commandments suit me,
      desire the things You forbid,
        and flirt with evil.
  Then I wonder, even when I get ahead,
    why I am not happy.

I have all kinds of things,
    but I am not content.
        My children are a pain.
        My job is a bore.
            My home is a battlefield.
I'm not sure I really want to live to old age.

I give You lip service,
    but not heart service.
I live in a world of fear—
    fear of the bomb,
        fear of the Russians,
            fear of the poor,
                fear of the muggers,
                    fear of the drug addicts,
                        fear of the murderers,
                            fear of the terrorists,
                                fear for the national debt,
                                    fear of losing my job,
                                        fear of death and futility.
I know what fear is!

But when I fear You,
    You dispel my restlessness and trepidation.
You help me to walk blithely through the ambushes of life.
    You fill my stomach,
        give me contentment,
            shower me with good,
                preserve my life,
                    and pacify my environment.
How much I need You, O Lord!
    How much I need You!

Fill me with the right kind of fear—
    awe before You, concern for Your approval—
        so that I may not cower before danger and uncertainty.
Bless me with the riches of Your peace
    so that my life may bless others with You!

AMEN

PSALM 129

O God, You have always preserved Your own.
  Though the history of Your nation, Israel,
    was one of constant oppression and opposition,
      yet You stood by her,
        and defended her,
          and gave her victory
            against overwhelming odds.
Her life was filled with suffering,
  with turmoil,
    with distress,
      and with difficulties of every kind.
But You were with her in all her trials,
  and You delivered her from the bonds
    of her enemies.

Father, may it be likewise in my life.
  May those who hate me because of my trust in You
    not be allowed to triumph over me.
  May my troubles be turned into occasions of moral victory.
    May the opposers and the oppressors
      receive neither Your blessing
        nor the encouragement of man.

O Father, there are many who hate You—
  who hate everything You are
    and everything You do.
Don't let them gain prominence or preeminence.
  Turn their evil plans to failure.
    Make their seeming success shortlived.
      Thwart their plots and undermine their power.
Cause them to wither,
  to waste away,
    to come to nothing.

Father, this is a day for me to rejoice
  as I contemplate Your love and care
    for Your children.

Rid my mind and heart of insecurity.
  Fill my thoughts with hope.
    Help me to meditate on Your glory.

Thank You for the truths of Your Word.
  I rejoice as I read the history of Israel.
    Thank You for involving Yourself in human affairs
      and for calling a people out from insignificance
        to be a chosen vessel of honor to Your name.

Give me courage today!
  Help me to realize that together,
    You and I can overcome any difficulty
      that presents itself.

Give me the confidence
  that comes from reliance
    on You in whatever difficulties
      enter my life!

AMEN

PSALM 130

O Lord, You know how often I have cried out to You.
　You have heard the prayer of my bewilderment,
　　my anguish,
　　　my despair,
　　　　my repentance,
　　　　　my longings,
　　　　　　and my fears.

Sometimes I feel like I am mired in the bottom of a deep pit,
　looking up at a small circle of sunlight
　　far, far away from me.
I feel alone,
　misunderstood,
　　unloved,
　　　unnecessary,
　　　　confused,
　　　　　and empty.

Sometimes I feel like a rock on the floor of a dark sea,
　washed continually by waves of despondency,
　　encrusted with the coral of doubt,
　　　ignored by those who sail by,
　　　　unimportant for any great purpose,
　　　　　plain,
　　　　　　useless,
　　　　　　　unnoticed,
　　　　　　　　insignificant,
　　　　　　　　　solitary,
　　　　　　　　　　and inert.

Then I lift my eyes and ears to You, O Lord.

I call out Your name,
　almost despairing of Your concern and presence.
I slowly form words of praise and supplication,
　my voice seems strange and hollow to my ears.

I call on you for deliverance.
   You hear my prayers.
   You listen to the yearnings of my heart,
     the anxiety of my mind,
       the despair of my spirit.
   You do not turn me off,
     or tune me out,
       or put me down.
   You envelop me with Your care;
     You cradle me with Your compassion;
       You bind up my wounds.

If You kept score,
   the number of my sins would be infinite.
   I would be condemned
     for the multitude
       of my transgressions.

I thank You that that is not Your way, O Lord.
   You are a God of forgiveness,
     renewal,
       salvation,
         and hope.

When I turn to You in fear and awe,
   the fearful and the awful things of my life
     melt away like the spring frost in the sun.
I need to learn to wait on You, Lord,
   to relax,
     to rest,
       to be quiet,
         to be patient,
           and to anticipate Your new day for my life.
I need to draw my truths from Your Word,
   to listen to the sounds of solitude,
     to meditate on your instructions,
       to listen for Your voice.
I need to de-bug the programs of my mind
   with the input of Your revelation, O Lord.

I wait for Your sunrise
   to dawn on the darkness of my night.
I watch as the black sky begins to turn gray,
   and the silhouettes of the horizon begin to take form,
     and the sky turns red with the promise of morning.
I wait,
   though I cannot wait,
     for the cold darkness to pass
       and the warmth and light of gladness to dawn.

You alone are my hope, O Lord.

You treat me with mercy,
   though I am sinful beyond measure.
You value me
   though I am filled with iniquity.
You are a God who knows,
   who cares,
     who hears,
       who forgives,
         who directs,
           who comforts,
             who restores,
               who redeems.

Help me today
       to rest
         once again
           in You.

AMEN

PSALM 131

Lord, I so need to learn humility.
  I often exalt myself and
    center all my thoughts on what brings
      me honor and praise.
  I need to keep myself in perspective,
    to realize that all that I am or have
      is because of Your grace in my life.

Please, Lord, help me to keep my eyes on You,
  instead of constantly focusing on myself
    and my desire to be somebody of importance.
Help me to keep my ambition in tune with Your will
  and to labor for the things that bring lasting happiness.
    Teach me to use my talents fully,
      but not to strive for things that I am
        incapable of handling.

Rather than prominence,
  give me contentment!
    I am so often like a fretting child
      hungry for its milk.
    I fuss and I squirm and I squall
      to have what I want, when I want it.
  Help me to rest quietly,
    contentedly,
      securely,
        happily in Your arms of love.

O Loving Father, You are my source of life and comfort.
  You give me significance.
    I don't need to exalt myself
      because You look out for my interests at every turn.
  You give me a sense of well-being and satisfaction.
    Help me to put my hope in You always!

AMEN

PSALM 132

Lord, You are a God who remembers.
You remember our humiliations,
our hard times,
and the times of our faithfulness.
You remember our vows,
our prayers,
our desire to honor You
in action as well as word.
It is good to be able
to enter into Your presence,
to serve Your purposes,
to worship before You,
to shout for joy,
to reflect Your desire for righteousness,
and to rely on You to bless Your chosen.

Your word to King David was sure.
He rose to the throne
and his descendants ruled from Mount Zion.
You honored His desire
that a house of worship might be built for You.
You lifted up Jerusalem
and made Your presence known
among the people.
You provided for their physical needs
and gave them joy in Your salvation.

Your blessing always rests on those
who keep Your covenant.
You chose to bless the world
through the seed of David.
You have given strength to David's house.
You have illuminated the world through Jesus.
He is King Eternal.

Thank You for fulfilling Your promises.

AMEN

PSALM 133

Dear Lord, I want the blessedness of unity.
I want to be united with You
so that my goals are Your goals
and so that my values are Your values.
So often I am at war with Your commandments
and Your will.
I want to be righteous,
but I flirt with sin.
I want to be holy,
but I blend in with the wicked.

O Lord, I seek harmony with those I love,
but I get angry,
and hurt, and vengeful.
I want peace,
but I create strife.
I long for someone to know me fully,
and care for me lovingly,
and understand me deeply,
and accept me wholly,
but I push some away,
and jab at others
with my thoughts and with my tongue.

True unity comes from You!
You give us ways to work together without compromise,
to comfort without judging,
to maintain relationships
when we want to run away.

Unity is a precious thing,
fragrant,
infectious,
refreshing,
healing.
It is like a hot bath on a December day,
a cool drink on an August afternoon.

Unity often seems static,
　but it is actually dynamic,
　　moving,
　　　developing,
　　　　outgoing,
　　　　　adjusting,
　　　　　　adapting,
　　　　　　　changing,
　　　　　　　　growing,
　　　　　　　　　working,
　　　　　　　　　　forgiving,
　　　　　　　　　　　renewing.
It brings peace to the mind,
　rest to the body,
　　health to the soul.

O God, bless me with completeness.
　Unite my fractured personality
　　from my head to my shoulders
　　　to the soles of my feet.
　Unite me within so that I may be united without.
　　Pour the ointment of Your oneness over me.
　　　Fuse me with other people of faith.
　　　　Enlist me in Your divine enterprise.
　　　　　Conform my will with Your will.
　Settle quietly over my discord.
　　Dissolve my fractious discontent.
　　　Transform my unstable temperament.
　　　　Silence my unruly tongue.
　Keep me from quarreling,
　　complaining,
　　　petifogging,
　　　　quibbling,
　　　　　disrupting,
　　　　　　squabbling,
　　　　　　　disputing,
　　　　　　　　feuding,
　　　　　　　　　wrangling,
　　　　　　　　　　gossiping,

Keep me from selfish reactions,
                fits of temper,
                    peevishness,
                        petulance,
                            irritability,
                            acerbity,
                                pugnacity,
                                    contentiousness,
                                    surliness,
                                        acrimoniousness,
                                    churlishness,
                                resentment,
                            anger,
                        revenge,
                    touchiness,
                huffiness,
            moodiness,
        crankiness,
    and capriciousness.

Bring symphony to the cacophony of my life,
    euphony to my ways.
        As water flows from the mountaintop,
            all unity flows from You, O God.
Oneness is Your blessing to the faithful and obedient.
    It gives hints of heaven,
        where the saints will dwell
            in perfect harmony forevermore.

Lord, give me a passion for unity—
    which is to say, of course,
        give me a passion for You!

AMEN

PSALM 134

I want to bless You, O Lord,
  by night
    and by day.
I am Your servant.
  I lift my thoughts
    in praise to You.
Help me to know
  what it really means for me to bless you.

I will come into Your presence
  in worship
    and open my lips in praise.
You created all that is.
  You shower blessings on the faithful.

Rain Your blessings on me.

AMEN

PSALM 135

How wonderful it is to praise You, O Lord.
When I think of You and Your attributes,
I find my heart is at peace
and my thoughts are filled with joy.
I join the great host of Your servants
in singing of Your goodness and might.

You chose the nation of Israel.
for a special people of Your own.
You revealed Yourself to them
and delivered them from oppression and bondage.
You surrounded them with signs and wonders.
You overcame their enemies
and gave them a land to call their own.

I am humbled, Lord, because You have also chosen me.

O Lord, You are very great.
There is nothing in all the universe
to compare with You.
You are sovereign
in the heavens
and on the earth.
You rule the seas and all the natural forces.
Even the weather is programmed by Your will.

Everything I know is in decay.
It is wearing out,
breaking down,
falling to pieces,
and going to ruin.

But Your name, O Father, endures forever.
Your fame is never diminished.
Your compassion never wanes.
Your love never ceases.

You are so unlike the idols I make for myself.
  They have no life,
    no personality,
      no compassion,
        and no divinity.
  Like inert wood and metal
    they are powerless to communicate,
      to act,
        to effect change,
          or to bring blessing.
  If I trust in them,
    my life will be just as dead and lifeless
    as they are.

But I exist to praise You, O true and living God.
  I unite with the chorus of the faithful
    to exalt and honor Your name.
Again and again my mind returns to the wonder
  of Your love and care for Your chosen ones.
You are good,
  great,
    awesome,
      wonderful,
        everlasting,
         genuine,
          living,
           and involved in my life.

O Lord, I praise Your holy name!

AMEN

PSALM 136

Lord, the Bible is filled with evidence
  that You are good and
    that Your love endures forever.
You created the universe
  and formed the features of the earth.
You put the sun and moon and stars
  in the heavens
    and appointed them to their tasks
    of illumination and splendor.

You called out a people unto You.
  You delivered the Hebrews from Egypt;
    You led them through the Red Sea;
      You destroyed their enemies behind them
      and before them.
You gave them the promised land to call their own.

All of these things demonstrate Your love and concern.
  Your everlasting compassion goes on and on.
    It reaches my generation with Your lovingkindness.
Just as You liberated Your people of old,
  You bring me freedom and life.
    You lift me up from obscurity and futility
    and make me heir to wonderful blessings.
  You defeat my enemies
    and free me from my sins.
  You sustain me with Your bounty
    and enfold me in Your everlasting love.

I lift my mind and heart to you
  in thanksgiving and praise,
    O God of heaven and earth!

AMEN

PSALM 137

Lord, I remember when days were better.
  I remember when I seemed in control of things.
    I remember when my life was filled
      with hope and promise.
How I sometimes long for the "good old days."
  I wish I could return to the simplicity of childhood.
    I long for the times when I felt at peace
      with myself and with You, O God.
I feel like a captive in an alien land,
  ill at ease,
    uncomfortable,
      afraid,
        anxious.
My heart aches;
  my eyes weep;
    my thoughts are confused;
      my songs are muted.

My tormentors want me to perform for them.
  My companions want me to pretend all is normal
    and as it should be.
But You know and I know
  that I am out of synch with my surroundings.
    I can't laugh anymore.
  I can't forget the things
    that once filled my life with meaning and purpose,
      but which now seem so far away and so long ago.

I don't want to forget You, O Lord.
  Don't let me feel at home
    in a place far from Your blessing.
  Don't let me settle for less than Your high standards.
    Don't let me forget You.
      Don't let me get comfortable with evil.
        Don't let me be satisfied
          with less than Your best for me.

I know that my life is in Your hands.
   I ask You to be my protector and avenger.
Don't let the things that seek my destruction prevail.
   Be at my side in the midst of the turmoil of my existence.
Help me to know that evil will be righted
   and that justice will prevail.
Help me to know that You are in control of human affairs.
   Help me to remember
      that You will bring down those who oppose You.

O Father,
   bring light to my darkness,
      hope to my depression,
         joy to my dreams,
            laughter to my relationships.

Help me to find my way back home to You,
   to the rest of Your presence,
      to the comfort of Your provision,
         to the haven of Your protection.

AMEN

PSALM 138

Lord, I will praise You with exuberance.
I want my heart and mind to be involved
as well as my tongue and lips.
My spirit is lifted up in song
as I contemplate Your greatness.

There is no other object or being worthy of my praise.
You are the focus of my adoration.
I love to gather with the faithful to praise You.
Your name is high above any other name
in heaven or on earth.
Your Word is true and holy forever.
Your love and faithfulness
are my constant contemplation.
I bow my head and heart to You,
O great and wonderful God.

You hear my prayers.
You give me strength to meet each day.
You make me secure and resolute.
You intervene on my behalf.

O that all people would praise You!
O that people of influence would exalt Your name.
O that people everywhere would listen for Your words,
and sing songs of Your marvelous ways,
and proclaim the news of Your great glory.

You are not influenced by reputations,
social standing,
or success.
You have a special love for the lowly and the needy.
In my times of trouble,
You preserve me.
In my times of fear and impotency,
You overcome my foes and lead me to victory.

O Lord, fulfill Your purpose for me.
Hold me close and wrap me in Your everlasting love.
Stay close beside me.
Keep my eyes on You every moment of every day.

AMEN

PSALM 139

O Lord God,
   You know me better than I know myself.
      The depth of Your knowledge
         is beyond any I can imagine.
      You know what I think, what I do, and why.

When I am walking, You are by my side.
   When I lie down, You watch over my bed
      like a young mother over her newborn child.
You know me inside and out.
   You know what I say,
      what I have said,
         and what I am going to say.
   You are a fortress before me,
      and behind me,
         and over me.

I marvel at all this.
   It boggles my mind.
      It is beyond my comprehension.
         I cannot understand it all.

There is no way for me to escape Your reality.
   I can take a rocket to the moon,
      and You are there before me.
   I can burrow into the depths of the earth,
      and You are there.
   I can sail to the remotest island,
      climb the highest mountain,
         or fly to the most distant star,
            but I will not escape Your presence
            or Your love.

You lead me like a father leads his child,
   reaching out to me with Your loving, strong hand,
      as I learn to walk through life.

From my conception to my death
    You are with me,
        guiding me,
            picking me up,
                cheering for me,
                    helping me,
                        wrapping me in Your love.
Night and day are alike to You.
    All things are known,
        seen, and understood.

When I look at my body,
    I am reminded that you made me.
        When I think of my inner nature,
            I am filled with awe.
You knew me when I was nothing more than a
    fertilized egg in my mother's womb.
You knew me before anyone else knew me,
    at the very moment
        when I began my journey of life.

How I yearn to know Your thoughts,
    Your truths,
        Your goodness.
O God, how marvelous is Your revelation to me!
    Your thoughts are beyond accounting.
        They encompass all that exists.
            They challenge my mind
                and extend my vision.

Let the wicked nature in me and others beware,
    for You are loving as well as just.
        It is no small thing
            to set oneself as Your enemy
                or to speak against Your name and works.

My heart grieves for those
    who do not truly know You.
        My spirit mourns for their wickedness.

O God, I lay myself open to You,
  knowing that You already know me,
    my motives,
      my thoughts,
        and my deeds.

Please, O Lord,
  keep me from sin
    and lead me in the way of life.

AMEN

PSALM 140

My Father, deliver me from the grasp of evil.
  Protect me from violence.
    Rescue me from the intrigues of my enemies.
      Keep me from the lies and slander of my foes.
Defend me from the hidden traps of the wicked.
  Preserve me in the midst of a world
    that seeks to deceive me.
Guard me from the dangerous philosophies,
  the man-centered wisdom,
    the trivial pursuits,
      and all the false gods
        of my time.

O Lord, help me to worship You only.
  You are my God.
    You hear my prayers.
      You deal with me in mercy.
        You deliver me from evil.
          You shield me from destruction.

O God, You humble the arrogant
  and thwart the desires of the wicked.
    I know that the sin of evil people
      comes to rest in their own lives.
They sow seeds of bitterness and hatred
  that grow into bumper crops of trouble and turmoil.
Their words of anger and rage return
  to poison all their relationships.
They plot to get even
  and are consumed by their own revenge.
They are constantly at war with someone.
  They find no rest or peace anywhere.
    They are stalked by disaster
      and racked by violence.
  They never find the peace
    of a tranquil home.

They carry within themselves
    their own destruction
        wherever they may be.
Father, don't let evil gain preeminence in my society.
    Don't let it get a foothold in my life.
        Give me a right sense of priorities.
            Help me to be more concerned for the good of others
                than I am for grudges or private gain.
    I know that You value the outcast,
        the underdog, the poor, the needy.
But Father, sometimes I find it so difficult
    to come to the aid of the ungrateful,
        the profligate,
            the user,
                the lazy,
                    the unmotivated,
                        and the undisciplined,
                            who so frequently ask for help
                                but refuse to listen to Your Word
                                    or welcome You into their lifestyles.

I know that You have called me to minister good
    to the people who surround me with wickedness.
        And quite frankly, Father,
            I just don't know how to do that.
    If I am generous,
        I feel guilty for allowing people to use me.
    If I am firm,
        I feel unloving and selfish.
    Friends and strangers
        come demanding time and attention
            I am loathe to give them.
    I have trouble relating to their needs,
        for I see habits that create those needs—
            things they do not wish to change.
    They manipulate me with their words,
        and no matter what I do,
            I feel uncertain and bewildered
                about what You would have me do.

But You have put me in this world
   to protect the poor and needy
      from the wicked and exploitive people
        who would prey upon them.
   You call on me to be an instrument of
   justice and compassion.

Give me, O Father,
   a sense of what is right.
Help me to praise You in my actions
   as well as my words.
Help me to live uprightly
   in the midst of this crooked and disjointed world.

Help me to sort through all the confusions
   of this tainted planet so that I can praise
      Your name with truth and righteousness!

AMEN

PSALM 141

O Lord, I need Your help right now.
  Listen to my prayer
    and respond to my needs.
May my prayers rise to You as sweet incense
  and may my uplifted hands manifest my devotion to You.

Take control of my mouth.
  Keep my lips from evil and
    from speaking maliciousness.
      Do not let me revel in depravity.
        Protect my lips from the food of folly
          and the drink of debauchery.
Don't let me become involved with evil enterprises.
  Keep me from desiring the favor of the ungodly.
    Don't let me compromise by
      becoming close with wicked men and women.
        Rather, make us uncomfortable with one another,
          as I pray continually against their sin.
Keep me from fraternizing with the enemy,
  from sitting down at the table of impurity,
    from enjoying the company of the depraved.
Keep me from desiring the wrong things,
  from adapting myself
    to the standards of my godless culture.
  Help me to discern evil and flee from it.
Stop me from accommodating
  to gain the approval of the unfaithful.

I'd rather be reproved by Your people
  than be comfortable among the unbelieving.
    Help me to seek the counsel of the virtuous
      and to encourage them to confront me with love.
    Their words of reproof are more valuable to me
      than the flattery of the sinful.
    Righteous words may wound me temporarily,
      but they produce health in the long run.

They teach me to persist in prayer
    even in the face of difficulty and defeat.
Those who love You learn through experience
    to trust You in every circumstance.

Help me to be aware of enticements to sin
    and to hate them with all my heart.

The wicked prosper for a time,
    but their days are numbered.
They will fall from their places of prominence,
    and their reputations and accomplishments
        will be shattered.
        They will be crushed,
            impoverished,
                splintered,
                    broken,
                        and displaced.

Though I sometimes feel
    like I am a car in a demolition derby,
I have learned to keep my eyes fixed on You, O God.
    Your approval is all I desire.
        You are the One in whom I can place my trust.
        You are my Savior and Deliverer.

Don't forsake me, O Lord.
    Don't abandon me to the schemes
        of the malevolent.
    Give me eyes to see the traps
        that lie in my path,
            to skirt the ambushes
                that threaten my safety in You.
    Help me to be wary,
        wise,
        and watchful.
    Cause the evil plans of the wicked
        to backfire on them
            while I escape their wicked devisings.

Hear me,
  protect me,
    separate me,
      correct me,
        vindicate me,
          preserve me,
            and deliver me,
O Lord, my God.

AMEN

PSALM 142

Lord, I'm so discouraged.
From the depths of my despair
I raise my feeble voice to You.
I call on you for tenderness,
for mercy,
for deliverance,
for strength,
for direction,
for protection,
for refuge,
and for understanding.

It relieves the pressure
just to be able to pour out to You
my pent-up frustration.
Though I am beset by so many difficulties right now,
You are very much on my mind as well.
Though I feel as if I'm not going to make it,
I know I can rely on You to lead me through
this time of trouble.

I can't put my trust in people.
When it gets right down to it,
they are more concerned for themselves
than for me.
Many of them are the source of my problems.
It's as if they were hunters
and I am the helpless animal
they seek to ensnare.
Rather than providing consolation
they treat me with indifference,
and sometimes with outright hostility.
They do not understand
or care.
But You are not like those who ignore and threaten me.
You are my source of deliverance.

You are my place of refuge.
　You are my protector.
　　You are the giver of life and freedom.

Please, Lord, listen to my prayer.
　I need Your help so desperately.
　　Bring me safely through this awful time.
　　　Give me strength to meet each difficulty.
　Don't let self-pity and depression overcome me.
　Liberate me from this gloom.

　Turn this dirge into a song of deliverance.
　　Transform my dire straits
　　　into a passage of peace.

But, Father, I will be sure to praise Your name,
　both now in the dark of my depression
　and after Your deliverance.
While covered by these shadows,
　and after they have been dispelled
　　by the light of Your love,
　　　I will lift my voice in thanksgiving.

The testimony of Your faithful lovingkindness toward me
　will be more compelling
　　because of what You have brought me through.
　My life will have a new effectiveness
　　because of my awareness of the goodness
　　　You have showered upon me.

I will find my place of service among Your people,
　and I will be able to minister to them
　　as You have ministered to me.

Lord, I feel better already.
　I began this prayer
　　thinking almost entirely of myself.
　　　But when I turned my mind and heart toward You,
　　　I began to think of the future with hope.

You have helped me to see a meaning
  in my present troubles.
You have shown me that they are equipping me
  in a very real way for service to You.
Thank You, Lord, for putting things back into perspective.
  I have learned once again that You are faithful.
    Help me not to forget this truth
      in the next upset of my life!

AMEN

PSALM 143

O Lord, I need Your help.
   Please listen to my prayer.
      You are faithful and righteous,
        and Your mercy is my hope,
          Your sovereignty my strength.
I come to You now,
    asking that You will relieve my anxiety and fear.
I am not worthy of Your concern.
    I know that.
But I cast myself before Your throne
    asking You to accept me as I am
      and to forgive me of my wayward ways.
I stand, not in my own righteousness,
    but in my faith in Your Son, Jesus Christ.

I am surrounded by foes.
   They grind me down
     and make my life a living death.
   I am weary
     and I am bewildered
       by the things that surround
         and threaten me.

My only hope is to think of the past.
   I know
     that You were with me in difficult times before.
   I know
     that You have come to my aid consistently
       and helped me through times as dark as this one.
   I long
     to fill my mind with Your benefits to me
      and rest in your goodness and might.
   I cannot get enough of You.
     I yearn for Your counsel;
       I reach out for Your blessing;
        I thirst for Your approval.

Please, Lord, hear my prayer.
    Come quickly to my aid
        for I am discouraged and anxious.
    If You do not intervene,
        I might as well be dead.
Let Your sunrise dawn on my dark night.
    Let Your unfailing love be manifest in this situation.
        You alone are my source of deliverance.
            I have put my trust in You,
                I know that You will not disappoint me.
                    You are the Lord God
                        and my Savior.

O Lord, show me the path I ought to follow.
    Reveal Your will so that I may walk in it.
        Guide my longing spirit in the path of faithfulness.
            Give me a teachable attitude
                and a faithful heart.

Rescue me, O Father, from the difficulties that surround me.
    Be my deliverance and my sanctuary.
        Hide me beneath Your everlasting love.
    You are my God,
        and I know You have planned everything
            for my good.
    With You at my side,
        I can meet life with confidence and tranquility.
You set my foot on the right path
    and lead me triumphantly through every trial.

I want my life to bear witness to Your glory, Lord.
    I want others to see Your power at work in my affairs.
        Keep me safe by means of Your righteousness,
            and bring me victoriously through every day.
    I want to be Your servant—
        to obey You,
            to honor You,
                to please You,
                    to do Your bidding daily.

You, I know, will watch over me with kindness.
    You will deliver me from my foes
        and protect me from my enemies.
    You will be my constant companion
        and will give meaning and purpose to my life.

O Father, I rest secure in Your unfailing love.

AMEN

PSALM 144

O Lord, You are my strength.
  You stand by me in every conflict.
  You are my fortress,
    my place of refuge,
    my deliverance,
      my protector,
      my strength,
        and my defender.

When I think of my pitiful strength
  and my lowly importance
    in the vast scheme of things,
      I marvel
        that You show any interest in me whatsoever.
It amazes me that You even know who I am.
  My life is so brief.
    so precarious,
      so fragile,
        so inconsequential—
          like a breath of air
          or a fleeting shadow.
Yet, You are concerned with human affairs
  —with my affairs.
You control nature for my benefit.
  You protect me by Your awesome might
    from those who oppose me.
  You save me from the turmoil of life
    and rescue me from the things
      that threaten to engulf me.
  You defend me from unknown dangers,
    from the slander of my enemies,
      from the power of evil.

It is appropriate that I thank You.
  It is well that I sing songs of praise,
    that I compose music of worship.

You are the one behind every victory.
  You are the author and sustainer of life.

Father, please deliver me,
  rescue me,
    defend me,
      vindicate me.
  Keep my mouth from vanity
    and let those who are proud
      know the falsehood of their vanity.

If You stand with me I will be blessed
  —fine children and abundant provisions
      are part of Your catalog of blessings.
  So are peace,
    freedom from fear,
      release from sorrow.
    May I honor You with my enterprises.
You are the source of every blessing.
  You are the provider for Your people.
    You are my God, my Lord, my King.
I find fulfillment and meaning in You!
  You are the source of joy,
    happiness,
      contentment.
I am complete because
  You are my God.

AMEN

PSALM 145

O God, You are my King.
  I will praise Your name forever.
Every day I exist gives me new reasons to adore You.
  Accept my grateful, loving worship.

O Lord, your greatness is beyond my understanding.
  My mind cannot comprehend it.
I have read in Scripture of Your mighty deeds.
  History proclaims Your greatness.
    Your wondrous works
      and the splendor of Your majesty
        give me reasons to praise You all day long.
  I see in Your character and in Your deeds
    expressions not only of Your power
      but also of Your goodness and righteousness.

You are gracious and compassionate,
  patient,
    merciful,
      loving,
        generous,
          slow to anger,
            faithful,
              worthy of praise.

Everything that exists praises You, O Lord.
  I join the chorus of the universe to extol You, O God.
    I want to proclaim Your greatness so that all may hear.
      I want to tell my parents,
        brothers,
          sisters,
            children,
              friends,
                neighbors,
                  co-workers,
                    of Your mighty acts.

I want the story of Your love
  to be passed on and on into the future,
    so that it will never be forgotten.

I want to celebrate Your greatness
  and sing of Your goodness and justice.
I join with all the saints who have gone before me
  to tell of Your glory
    and proclaim the chronicles of Your power.
I have experienced the wonder of Your mighty acts.
  I have seen the majestic splendor of Your kingdom.

You and Your kingdom are everlasting,
  Your rule goes on and on without end.

Your promises are true, O Lord.
  Your love is steadfast.
    You reach down and restore those who are faint.
    You steady those who stumble;
      You encourage the discouraged;
        You provide for the hungry and needy;
          You replenish the exhausted and downcast.

All living things look to You for their needs.
  You satisfy all their desires from Your open hand.
    Your timing is always perfect.
  You are righteous in all Your ways,
    gracious and loving in all Your deeds.
  You are near me when I call out to You,
    merciful and tender in Your answers.
      Help me to call upon You in truth and trust.

You are a God who watches over those who love You.
  You will not allow wickedness to triumph.
    You create and fulfill the fondest desires
      of those who worship You
        in respect and reverence.
  You answer their prayers and save them.
    You lift up those who are burdened.

Father, when I think of these things,
  I am overcome with awe.
    My mouth overflows with words of praise.
      My mind ponders Your mighty works.
        My heart responds in love.
    My body experiences the wholeness of Your blessings,
      My spirit joins the adoration ringing through all creation
      to praise Your holy name forever and ever.

Praise the Lord!
  Praise the Lord!
    Praise the Lord!
      Praise the Lord!
        Praise Your holy name!

AMEN

PSALM 146

Praise the Lord!
Oh let me praise You, Lord,
  with my deepest concentration,
    with my innermost feelings,
      with my strongest impulses.
Let the whole of my life be a praise to You.
  Let me fill my days with thanksgiving
    and my nights with reflections on Your goodness.
  Let my hope be Your presence
    and my song be Your greatness.
  Let me be filled
    with the joy of Your love
      and the changelessness of Your mercy.
While I draw breath to live
  may I expel words of praise to You!

I'm often tempted to trust human powers
  and governments for my security.
I'm prone to think that other people
  can give meaning to my life.
But human institutions and human beings
  are just as mortal and uncertain as I am.
Men take pride in their great power,
  and their great theories,
    and their great discoveries,
  but before long
    the powerful are dead,
      the theories are discarded,
        and the discoveries are obsolete.

But You, O God, are not like mortal men.
  All things come from You.
    You made the heavens
      and the earth
      and the sea
        and all that fly, roam, and swim in them.

Your truth is always powerful,
   always relevant,
     always trustworthy.
You are my source of happiness,
   my spring of hope,
     my door of expectation.

I can trust You
   with the things I cannot understand—
     injustice,
       famine,
         abortion,
           handicaps,
             drug abuse,
               oppression,
                 illness,
                   prejudice,
                     estrangement,
                     suffering,
                       immorality,
                       wickedness,
                       pain,
                       sorrow.
I can trust Your justice and sovereign will.
   I need not despair.

My grand designs fail,
   and their greatness is buried with them.
You, though, make no futile plans or false starts.
   You are eternally faithful and true.
     You care for every need of the humanity You created.
   You love the righteous.
   You look after the stranger.
     You protect the orphan ... and the elderly.
You frustrate the evil purposes of the wicked.
   You judge with absolute righteousness.

You will rule forever!
   Reign in my heart, O Lord!

I will simply,
 lovingly,
  joyously,
   confidently,
    exuberantly,
     resolutely,
      triumphantly,
       consistently
        praise You, Lord.

This is my purpose, my only purpose, Lord—
 to praise You.
  I will do it as long as You allow me to live.
There is no one but You who is worthy of my worhsip.

Please accept my praise, my magnificent God!
 Let all those I know join me in praising You.
We praise You, Lord!

AMEN

PSALM 147

O Father, I want to sing a song of Your greatness.
I want to meditate upon Your majesty.
I know it is right to give You praise.

You bring Your people together in gladness.
You heal the brokenhearted.
You bind up the wounded.
You sustain the humble.
You bring peace to the faithful.
You give direction to the obedient.

There is no limit to Your knowledge and power.
All of nature is under Your control.
You know the number and the names of all the stars.
You control every weather pattern.
Your word sends the snow
and hurls the hail,
and initiates the ice,
and fabricates the frost,
and triggers the thaw.
You provide for every bird and animal.
You give the fields their harvest.
You supply the beasts their food.

But You take more delight in my obedience
than in the whole of Your twinkling night sky.
You are more concerned about my faith
than about the world's intricate ecology.
You delight in me
when I put my confidence in Your unfailing love.
You joy in my trusting response
to Your unfailing concern.
I want to add to my song
the refrain of thanksgiving.
I want to add lyrics of homage
giving You all glory.

O God, I want to praise You
    for Your goodness to the faithful.
        You give us personal worth and security.
          You grant peace and satisfaction.
            You reveal Your desires through Your Word.
            You treat us as very important persons.

Father, everywhere I look I see reminders of Your loving care.
Thank You for revealing Your nature and will to me.
    Give me a heart of obedience and faithful praise.

AMEN

PSALM 148

Father, when I praise You,
  I join in the chorus of the cosmos!
    The host of Your angels add their voices
      of praise to the song of the physical world.
    The heavens declare Your creative magnificence.
      The sun, moon, and stars shout of Your greatness.
      The sky screams of Your glory.

Everything You have made
  —and that means everything that is—
    praises You!

I see the sun rising each morning
  and setting each evening.
    I see the moon reflecting sunlight
    into my night sky.
      I see the stars sending their radiance to me
        across eons of light years,
          and I am reminded of Your greatness,
            honored through the whole of creation.
I think of the remarkable way
  water falls from the heavens,
    cascades down mountain streams
      into mighty rivers,
        empties into the great seas,
          and then evaporates back into the sky
        where the wonderful cycle
          begins all over again.

Everything in this intricately planned environment
  is designed by Your mind
    and brought into existence by Your word.
      You put everything in its place
        and gave it a uniformity
          that allows me to study it
            and work with it for my benefit.

At Your command the universe came into existence.
  By Your firm decree,
    You hold the planets in their place.
You created the earth and all its inhabitants,
  from the smallest coral creature to the mightiest whale,
    from the lion to the lamb,
      from the gnat to the eagle,
        from the slave to the king,
          from the young child to the senior citizen,
            from the baby to the octogenarian,
              from the famous to the obscure,
                from the powerful to the weak.

You make the lightning,
  the hail,
    the snow,
      the fog,
        the clouds,
          the wind,
            the heat,
              the rain,
                the cold,
                  the sunshine,
                    the gentle breeze,
                      the icebergs,
                        the drought,
                          the tides.

Your splendor is above all the earth.
  Your glory is sounded forth from the heavens.
You bless Your chosen with fullness.
  You honor Your saints with Your fellowship.

The ocean swarms with millions of creatures,
  infinite in variety and design.
The world speaks of Your greatness.
  The mountains and hills,
    along with the forests and orchards,
      proclaim Your glory.

All flora and fauna praise Your majesty.
   Lions,
      and tigers,
        and bears,
          and hippos,
            and whooping cranes,
              and emus,
                and elephants,
                  and Guernsey cows,
                and sheep,
                  and hogs,
                    and chickens,
                    and turkeys,
                    and ducks,
                    and geese,
                    and owls,
                      and rabbits,
                      and dogs,
                      and cats,

and Clydesdales,
  and donkeys,
    and oxen,
      and sparrows,
        and robins,
          and lightning bugs
        and clams,
          and silkworms,
        and goats,
          and cheetahs,
            and koala bears,
          and wallabies,
            and hornbills,
            and martins,
              and katydids,
            and snails,
              and octopuses,
                and crocodiles,
              and eagles,
                and chipmunks,

and wombats,
and longhorn steers,
and moles,
and possums,
and raccoons,
and turtles,
and muskrats,
and seals,
and minks,
and camels,
and cardinals,
and gulls,
and wildebeests,
and otters,
and lobsters,
and gazelles,
and ermine,
and Shetland ponies,
and hamsters,
and canaries,
and mockingbirds,
and woodpeckers,
and ground hogs,
and ospreys,
and gibbons,
and greyhounds,
and bees,
and okapis,
and rhinos,
and chimps,
and beagles,
and parrots,
and armadillos,
and blue jays,
and collies,
and wolves,
and pandas
and mice,
and squirrels.

and gnus,
  and bats,
    and butterflies,
      and salmon,
        and penguins,
          and flamingos,
          and giraffes,
          and shrimp,
          and starfish,
           and ostriches,
            and kangaroos,
              and thoroughbreds,
            and foxes,
          and ants,
          and huskies,
          and dolphins—
PRAISE YOUR HOLY NAME!

Help me, Father, to worship You as I ought.
  Help me to make You supreme in my life.
    Help me to see Your splendor
    in all You have created.
Thank You for holding me close to Your heart.
  Thank You for desiring my praise.
    Thank You for reminding me
    of my origin in You
      and my destination with You.
Thank You for allowing me
  to join the glad song of praise
    that reverberates through the whole of creation.

All political systems,
  and politicians,
    and governors,
      and congresses,
        and legislatures,
          and parliaments,
        and kingdoms,
          and presidents,

and kings,
  and prime ministers,
    and rajahs,
      and chiefs,
        and emperors,
          and potentates,
            and princes
              owe You honor and glory.
All people—
  young and old,
    men and women,
      high and low,
        wise and foolish,
          learned and uneducated,
            famous and obscure,
              rich and poor,
                cultured and uncultured,
                  are subject to Your holy name.

All nature does Your bidding—
  storms,
    blizzards,
      monsoons,
        typhoons,
          tornadoes,
            avalanches,
              sleet,
                cyclones,
                  thunder,
                    gales,
                      and hurricanes.
      all come and go according to Your plan.

Your name is above all others.
  Your glory shines in the heavens.
    Your nature is supreme and holy.
    Your wisdom is unsurpassed.
      Your imagination is beyond my imagining.
      Your splendor is eternal.

How grateful I am that You take notice of me.
  I thank You for having concern for my affairs.
    I thank You for wanting me to add
      my little words of
        praise and thanksgiving
          to the hosannah of the universe.
Thank You for drawing me close to Your heart in Christ Jesus.
  Thank You for the grace and love
    that allow me to call You my God.

I exalt You.
  I need You.
    I want You.
      I celebrate You.
      I love You.
        I praise You.

AMEN

PSALM 149

I come to adore You, O Lord.
  I come to sing You a song of newness and delight.
    I come to magnify You in the assembly of the saints.
      I come to praise Your name with joy.
        I come to make music with tambourine and harp.

O let all Your people join me
  in glad words and songs of homage.
    Let us rejoice in the praise of You—our Creator.
      Let us be glad in the majesty of You—our divine King.

O how wonderful it is to bask in Your approval.
  You delight in providing good.
    You reward the humble with deliverance.
      You bring the joy of contentment
        and the peace of fulfillment.

I will sing songs of praise both day and night.
  My mouth will be filled with words of adoration.
    My life will be dedicated to Your cause.
  My thoughts will be focused on honoring Your name.
    My words will be uttered to discomfit the wicked.
      My strength will be expended for Your glory.

I will labor as Your instrument of righteousness.
  I will dedicate myself to the fulfillment of Your will.
    I will glorify You in every idea and action.

Oh, how wonderful it is to sing and shout to You.
  How good it is
    to join the chorus of the heavens
      in exuberant praise.
        How satisfying it is to glorify Your name
          in the company of the saints.
  I rejoice in the praise of my Maker!
    I am glad in the majesty of my King!

AMEN

PSALM 150

O Lord, I love to honor You.
  I delight in joining the chorus of the heavens
    in a glad song of love and adoration.
  I long to meditate on Your deeds of might.
    I yearn to think deeply of Your strength and glory.

O God, Your greatness is everlasting.
  Your power is incomparable.
    Your wisdom is beyond imagining.

Every musical instrument adds its special note of praise.
  Wind instruments blast forth Your glory.
    Stringed instruments resonate Your majesty.
      Percussion instruments sound forth Your omnipotence.

I delight in the great crescendo of praise.
  I hear a symphony in full chorus.
    Let trumpets,
      harps,
        lyres,
          tambourines,
            flutes,
              cymbals,
                and gongs praise You.
  Let electric guitars,
    and synthesizers,
      and kettle drums,
        and violins,
          and trombones,
            and oboes,
              and French horns,
                and snare drums,
                  and xylophones,
                    and marimbas,
                      and saxophones,
                    and tubas,

and clarinets,
　and pianos,
　　and organs,
　　　and basses,
　　　　and six-stringed guitars,
　　　　　and banjos,
　　　　　　and ukeleles,
　　　　　　　and zithers,
　　　　　　　　and bagpipes,
　　　　　　　　　and bongo drums,
　　　　　　　　　and cowbells,
　　　　　　　　　　and piccolos,
　　　　　　　　　　and cornets,
　　　　　　　　　　　and bugles,
　　　　　　　　　　　　sound forth.

In a swelling orchestra of devotion, O Lord,
　may everything that draws breath praise You!

Thank You for giving us the gift of music.
　It quiets our tensions,
　　excites our feelings,
　　　and reflects Your creativity.
　But most of all,
　　it provides a way to express
　　　love and adoration to You.

May the music of my thoughts,
　my lips,
　　and my hands
　　　praise You
　　　　from the deepest
　　　　　recesses of my heart!

AMEN